S0-BBM-823

*The Know Nothing Party in New Orleans*

Leon Cyprian Soulé

# *The Know Nothing Party in New Orleans:*

## A REAPPRAISAL

*Published by*
The Louisiana Historical Association

*To Lucile*

Copyright 1961 by
The Louisiana Historical Association
Library of Congress Catalog Card Number: 61-18381
Manufactured in the United States of America by
Thomas J. Moran's Sons, Inc., Baton Rouge

# *Preface*

ALMOST from its inception the New Orleans Know Nothing party stood for principles different than those for which the national party was founded. The local organization was never a legitimate offspring of the parent, despite ardent protests of loyalty by New Orleans members. Although much has been written about the party in the Crescent City, its local idiosyncrasies, which were its reason for being, have heretofore been left unnoticed. Yet, for nearly ten years the politics of New Orleans and, to some extent, Louisiana was radically affected by the peculiar course of Know Nothingism in the city. This volume does not purport to be a detailed history of the party's activities; this ground has already been covered. It is rather a reappraisal in which the emphasis is laid on political behavior. It grew out of a desire to understand why this short-lived phenomenon of American political history kept New Orleans in its grasp even after the chaos of war had engulfed its rivals.

I should like to express my appreciation to the staffs of the Howard-Tilton Library of Tulane University and the New Orleans Public Library for their kind assistance. To Charles P. Roland, Gerald M. Capers, and Robert C. Reinders I shall always be grateful for their painstaking reading and criticism of the manuscript. Lastly, I thank my wife for devotion beyond the call of duty.

L.C.S.

New Orleans, Louisiana
August 8, 1961

# *Table of Contents*

# *Illustrations*

*The Know Nothing Party in New Orleans*

CHAPTER ONE

# Of Creoles, Americans, and Politics

AFTER the collapse of the Whig party in the early 1850's many of its former members were absorbed into a new political structure—the Native Americans or Know Nothings. Slavery had wrecked the party of Henry Clay, and the founders of Native Americanism were determined to avoid this issue. Antiforeignism and anti-Catholicism were the chief planks of the Know Nothing platform. Coming at a time when no national organization could ignore slavery and survive, the party was destined to a short life. Formed about 1853, it was practically eradicated after its abortive effort to elect Millard Fillmore president in 1856.

In New Orleans, however, the Know Nothing party achieved some of its most outstanding victories after 1856. Far from dying, it was the dominant political force until the invasion of the city by the Federal troops in April of 1862. Chroniclers of the party's history in Louisiana and New Orleans have all expressed surprise over this phenomenon, but none have explained it.[1] The answer lay in the cultural and political battles between the Creoles and the Americans.

The population of New Orleans in the 1850's was divided into three groups. First, there were the Latin Creoles, the French and Spanish families of the colonial period and their descendants. The second group contained the Anglo-Americans

[1]W. Darrell Overdyke, "History of the American Party in Louisiana," *Louisiana Historical Quarterly*, XV (October, 1932), 581–88; XVI (January, April, July, October, 1933), 84–91, 256–77, 409–26, 608–27; Edith Chalin Follett, "The History of the Know Nothing Party in Louisiana" (unpublished master's thesis, Tulane University, 1910).

who came after the Louisiana Purchase in 1803 and their descendants. Last, there were the European immigrants—the Irish, Germans, and French—who came to New Orleans in large numbers toward the middle of the nineteenth century.

Political orientation was generally along the same lines, except for the Latin Creole group, which was augmented by the "foreign" French and some Anglo-Americans. These Anglo-Americans became identified with the Creoles usually through intermarriage or by association. Especially was this true of those families who came soon after the Purchase. The "foreign" French joined the Creoles because language and love of France naturally brought them together. The term Creole as herein employed is used to designate a political combination, although some of the individuals were Creoles only in this special sense: they wished to see the French municipality dominate. The Creoles and Americans had been fighting each other long before the arrival of the Irish and Germans. As the immigrant group increased in size, it came to hold the balance of power between the other two.

Many of the Anglo-Americans, who came in large numbers during the decades after the Purchase, were culturally incompatible with the Creoles and settled a new section of the city above Canal Street. Antagonisms increased with the years, and disputes over how the city should be governed led to the division of New Orleans into three separate municipalities in 1836. Economic necessity forced a reunion in 1852, but the differences between the two groups were not erased by legislative enactment.

With the reunification of the city's government it was natural that both Creoles and Americans would seek to find ways to dominate. Each had to build a political organization or machine behind which to muster its forces. The Americans lined up behind the Whigs, but as that party died within a year after reunification, they turned their support to the Know Nothings. The Creoles generally voted Democrat. Toward the end of the 1850's both parties split and the classifications no longer held. Even in the beginning of the decade many uptown Americans voted Democrat and many downtown Creoles voted Whig and then Know Nothing. Therefore, neither group would label itself Creole nor American, downtown nor uptown. To have done so would have lost it many valuable votes.

Reappraising the Know Nothings in New Orleans as a front behind which the Americans fought the Creoles is difficult because of this lack of positive party identification. Support for such a thesis must of necessity come in part from some material which antedates the actual formation of the party. Ostensibly, the reunification of 1852 marked the end of cultural antagonism. After that, no one would deliberately put himself in a position where he could be accused of opening old wounds. But if there were deep-seated antagonisms before 1852, certainly they continued afterwards. Such deductive evidence is by no means sufficient proof of the thesis, but in the light of later lack of public pronouncement it is important evidence.

Students of New Orleans in the 1850's disagree as to the extent to which Creole-American animosities existed. One has concluded that "whatever the ethnic cleavages might have been in the early history of the city, differences between the Creole and American had nearly disappeared by 1850—if not earlier."[2] Another has seen the conflict in terms of class.[3] Although both views are misleading, even more confusing is the comment of the contemporary historian and politician, Charles Gayarré, who, in his address to the New York Know Nothing convention of 1855, also expressed the opinion that most Creole-

[2]Robert Clemens Reinders, "A Social History of New Orleans, 1850–1860" (unpublished Ph.D. dissertation, The University of Texas, 1957), I, 150. In the chapter entitled "Social Classes" Dr. Reinders cites such sources as Henry A. Murray, *Lands of the Slave and the Free; or Cuba, the United States, and Canada* (London, 1857); J. J. Ampère, *Promenade en Amerique* (Paris, 1855); Lillian Foster, *Way-Side Glimpses North and South* (New York, 1860); and some church records. He does prove the existence of some Creole-American business enterprises and intermarriages. These alone, however, do not sufficiently support the thesis that antagonism had disappeared, in view of abundant evidence to the contrary.

[3]Roger W. Shugg, *Origins of Class Struggle in Louisiana* (Baton Rouge, 1939), 31, 146.

American hostility was gone by the 1850's.[4] Gayarré was hardly reliable on this score. Believing himself to have been wronged by the Democrats, he joined in protest the party which was chiefly the instrument of the Americans in their fight with the Creoles. Thorough Creole that he was, he might well have justified such renegade action by minimizing the antipathy between the two cultures during that era. Certainly the facts regarding New Orleans politics in the 1850's do not bear out Gayarré's comments on Creole-American relations.

George Washington Cable, who lived in New Orleans during the 1850's, argues quite to the contrary. In the *Social Statistics of Cities*, a part of the Census of 1880, Cable concludes that in most American cities the foreign element was inspired to become Americanized but that such was not the case in New Orleans. "In New Orleans," he says, "the American thought was foreign, and not only foreign but unwelcome. The American found himself in the minority of a social situation which was more in sympathy with European ideas than those of the New World." The Creoles, he continues, retained much power both by their natural force and by their extensive ownership of real estate. Also, an easily formed coalition with foreign elements helped to keep them in this position. When the Creoles realized that they could no longer dictate public sentiment, they became divided and met most imperative necessities for innovation with inflexible conservatism.[5]

Alfred Mercier, a typical Creole whose writings are extant, harbored distrust and outright fear of his Anglo-Saxon rival. "In one wink of the eye that [section] . . . took the proportions of a suburb, and now the suburb is a city with a vast port, churches, hotels, verandas, theatres, etc. And it is that city juxtaposed to ours, which will end by absorbing and annihilating us, if we do not take care; for its port stops the goods

[4]Follett, "The History of the Know Nothing Party in Louisiana," 55.

[5]George Washington Cable, "New Orleans, Historical Sketch," *Report on the Social Statistics of Cities*, George E. Waring, Jr., comp. (United States Bureau of Census, *Tenth Census of the United States: 1880*, XIX [Washington: Government Printing Office, 1887]), 257.

which come down the river before they arrive at ours, and already we see the ships . . . ascend toward the new anchorage where there is greater activity."[6] Although Mercier was writing in the late 1840's, it is not likely that the constantly increasing numbers of Americans lessened the fears of people like him.

The famous English traveler and scientist, Sir Charles Lyell, noted that the differences between the Creoles and Americans were distinct and that each seemed to get on the other's nerves. On a trip from the mouth of the river to New Orleans he observed that the boat was stopped several times in order that hogsheads of sugar could be taken aboard or repaired or that a French plantation owner could be picked up who was late getting to the landing. Lyell says of one such incident, "I observed that all those whose native tongue was English were indignant at the small barrier which the captain seemed to set on their time; but the Creole majority, who spoke French, were in excellent humor." The Americans spoke of attempting to discipline the French in respect to keeping people waiting, and Lyell reports overhearing a conversation in which an American berated the French because "they retain all their antiquated usages, seeming to hate innovation." In discussing politics, Lyell stated that "a Creole always voted for a Creole candidate at an election, however much he differed from his political opinions, rather than support an Anglo-Saxon of his own party." Lyell thought that he would be tempted to do the same if he were of French origin and heard his race as much run down as were the Creoles of Louisiana.[7]

[6]Alfred Mercier, *Biographie de Pierre Soulé* (Paris, 1848), 40. My translation of: "En un clin d'oeil cette . . . prit les proportions d'un faubourg, et maintenant le faubourg est une ville avec un vaste port, des églises, des hôtels, des vérandas, des théâtres, etc. Et c'est cette ville juxta-posée à la nôtre, qui finira par nous absorber et nous annihiler, si nous n'y prenons garde; car son port arrête les marchandises qui descendent le fleuve avant qu'elles n'arrivent au nôtre, et déjà nous voyons les navires, . . . monter vers le nouvel ancrage où bouillonne plus d'activité."

[7]Sir Charles Lyell, *A Second Visit to the United States* (London, 1849), II, 156–57.

Another writer also notes that the Louisiana French and Americans often opposed each other regardless of political party affiliation—that the Anglo-Americans looked down on Creoles of their own party because they were "constitutionally opposed to development and progress." The Creoles "kept themselves together with a reserve and exclusiveness almost impenetrable." The same historian even believed that Creole-American differences were pronounced as late as 1890,[8] but he never saw in these differences a clue to the tangled politics of the period.

Another intimation that Creole-American hostility had political consequences is found in the section of *Biographical and Historical Memoirs of Louisiana* written by Frank McGloin. In describing the effects of the separation of the municipalities, McGloin says that "the second [American] municipality prospered in proportion as the other two districts declined in commercial importance. The anomalous condition of three cities in one, with *varied and hostile interests* [italics mine] each suffering from financial embarrassments was found to be not conducive to permanent prosperity as a city, and in 1852 the three municipalities were again consolidated into one city government."[9] Hostile and varied interests do not produce political harmony.

Other writers working in nonpolitical areas of New Orleans history have also come to the conclusion that there was conflict between the Americans and the Creoles in the 1850's. Ben Avis Adams, who in 1939 wrote a study of the assimilation of the Creole people of New Orleans, concluded that there was Creole-American conflict until the Civil War, and his conclusion seems to be borne out by several case studies he made in the course of his work.[10] Edward L. Tinker in his *Creole City* also concludes that the two cultures were not fused during the

[8]James Kimmins Greer, "Louisiana Politics, 1845–1861," *Louisiana Historical Quarterly*, XII (July, 1929), 387–88, 391.

[9]Frank McGloin, "History of New Orleans," *Biographical and Historical Memoirs of Louisiana* (Chicago, 1892), I, 184–85.

[10]Ben Avis Adams, "Indexes of the Assimilation of the Creole People in New Orleans" (unpublished master's thesis, Tulane University, 1939).

period of the 1850's and that it took the Civil War to get them together.[11]

Additional evidence of antipathy between the two is found in the writings of a group of authors in the 1890's who could be called "professional New Orleans Creoles." This group would defend the Creoles against any and all attackers. They grew up during that era in New Orleans history when the Creoles' power was fast slipping away. Outstanding among these writers are Grace King *(Creole Families of New Orleans)* and Henry Castellanos *(New Orleans As It Was)*. In discussing the Americans' participation in politics, King says that they were "trained to perfection in the skillful manipulation of municipal patronage for private profit." Writing late in the nineties, she still maintained that "Jackson Square still reigns, the center of all civic, social and ecclesiastical functions of ceremony."[12] Henry Castellanos, a New Orleans Creole youth during the Know Nothing episode of the 1850's, writes of that period with a tone that is not merely indicative of lack of sympathy for a political party. He shows real hatred for a group. In speaking of Governor Robert Charles Wicliffe's refusal to pardon a Know Nothing convicted of murder, he says, "The Hercules that had strangled the hydra of Know Nothingism in Louisiana two years before" would not pardon him.[13] Oftentimes these "professional Creoles" speak of the Americans who opposed their ancestors as almost treacherous.

Historical evidence indicates that during the 1850's Canal Street was still the boundary between French and American New Orleans. The press often made remarks indicative of the division, as occurred when the New Orleans *Weekly Delta* said on February 22, 1852, "People will now have no reluctance to living in one portion or another of the city because of its being the 'French' or the 'American' part of the city."

[11]Edward L. Tinker, *Creole City* (New York, 1953), 60.

[12]Grace King, *Creole Families of New Orleans* (New York, 1921), 128.

[13]Henry Castellanos, *New Orleans As It Was* (New Orleans, 1895), 110–14.

The opinion of the *Delta* was premature, however, for such prejudices do not die by legislation.

Evidence that the Vieux Carré was still essentially a French city is supported by the researches of Nathaniel C. Curtis. His investigations show that the French Quarter as we know it today was built between 1800 and 1850, with many of the houses constructed in the decade of the 1850's. He notes that this building occurred approximately at the same time as that of many houses of the Garden District, yet architecturally the two are unalike. He attributes this factor to the different people who built and inhabited each section—the Americans in the Garden District and the Creoles in the French Quarter.[14]

That New Orleans was not a unified city in the 1850's is also well attested by a northern governess who spent the early years of the decade there. "There are two distinct cities," she says, "that make up New Orleans—the American and French. The former is so much like a Northern city that I did not remain in it much, although the most superb portion; but I took kindly to the latter for its very novelty. In the French part, few of the population speak English. Their language, manners, customs, are preserved; and a Parisian would think himself in a city of France, if he did not cross Canal Street, which is the Rubicon that separates the American quarter from it. In walking through the French municipality, or district, I could hardly realize that I was in my native land."[15]

Perhaps the most reliable source of information as to who lived where in New Orleans in the 1850's and 1860's can be found in the United States Census of those decades. An examination reveals that the French Quarter in the fifties was inhabited mainly by people born in either Louisiana or France. The uptown district, the second (American) municipality, was

[14]Nathaniel C. Curtis, *New Orleans; Its Old Houses, Shops and Public Buildings* (Philadelphia, 1933), 118.

[15]Joseph Holt Ingraham, *The Sunny South, or the Southerner at Home, Embracing Five Years' Experience of a Northern Governess in the Land of the Sugar and the Cotton* (Philadelphia, 1860), 348.

inhabited largely by people born in other states of the Union, especially New York. The statement that the French Quarter was essentially French while the American district was essentially American is statistically correct. Of course, some Americans did live in the French Quarter, and a few French lived uptown.

Even while New Orleans was separated into three municipalities with each virtually governing itself, the Creoles and Americans never missed an opportunity to undermine each other's positions. In the Louisiana constitutional convention of 1845 several of the debates and issues involved had to do with the intracity struggle rather than with matters of statewide concern. On the question of setting the day for elections, the Creoles, led by Bernard Marigny and Pierre Soulé, held out for a date during the summer when many Americans left New Orleans because of the threat of yellow fever. Marigny said that a loyal citizen did not flee because of fear of a disease, but stuck it out and was thereby baptized into true citizenship in Louisiana.

The Americans accused the Creoles of acting purely from local feeling, and Christian Roselius answered Marigny that he saw absolutely no relationship between leaving the city because of yellow fever and being deprived of one's right to vote. Roselius made it clear that he understood Marigny's intention, which was to disfranchise that large segment of the population of New Orleans which left the city every summer, and he denied that yellow fever constituted a baptism into citizenship, as Marigny had claimed. Roselius insisted that "birds of passage," to which Marigny had referred, certainly could not vote anyway and that these "birds," as Marigny well knew, would include Americans as well as unauthorized voters. Roselius admitted that there were numerous visitors present in the city in the spring who were not entitled to vote, but who might try. Nevertheless, he would not permit a large part of the population to be disfranchised by setting the election date in September, especially when so doing would affect a group who he thought were involved in the prosperity of the state "as much as any other portion of the community."[16]

Charles M. Conrad of New Orleans questioned the motives of the whole committee which recommended the September date for elections. He insisted that, if the "birds of passage" as Marigny called them were present in May, they would also be present in September, for they lacked the means to escape the city. To Conrad the real implication of the measure was, therefore, to eliminate a group of qualified American voters. Marigny answered Conrad by saying that the suggestion was not the whole committee's, but simply his own; in other words, that it was strictly a New Orleans quarrel.[17]

When George Eustis, an American of New Orleans, arose to address the convention, he boldly declared that fixing the time of elections was "nothing more nor less than a question of political power. Before that issue all other considerations sink into insignificance." Eustis said further that those men who venerated the old constitution which they had written, obviously referring to the Creoles, should show a little more of that veneration now and not quarrel so much over the date, but leave it where it was originally set, in July. (Apparently the Americans stayed in New Orleans through early July.)

Pursuing the same argument, John C. Beatty, a Democratic delegate from New Orleans, made the case even stronger when he declared that the question of setting the time of election was not only a question of political power but that he had evidence which would prove this point. At the time of the last election in New Orleans in 1845, according to Beatty, the second municipality (American section) had returned a higher vote than the first and third combined, when everybody knew that the latter two had a higher population. His implication was that much illegal voting must have been going on in the second municipality. Extra American votes were exactly what Marigny sought to eliminate. If the election were held at a

[16]*Journal of the Constitutional Convention, 1845* (New Orleans, 1845), 20–21.

[17]*Ibid.*, 38.

time when the American section was empty, the other two stood a better chance to dominate.

Other delegates to the convention from the country parishes said that the elections should be "free from all quirks and undue influence" and that local feeling should never actuate any delegate in setting the time of the election.[18] But the real issue at hand was expressed by Eustis and Beatty when they openly contended that political power was the motivating force in determining an election date.

The other major Creole-American clash in the convention of 1845 came over setting the time a naturalized citizen had to wait before he could vote. Newly arrived Americans who were not legally qualified because they had not lived in the city long enough often voted. With the arrival of large numbers of foreign immigrants, who had more in common with the French than with the American elements of the population of New Orleans, the Creoles had a chance to redress this unfavorable balance—if these fresh arrivals could vote. The Creoles, therefore, advocated allowing immigrants to vote one year after becoming naturalized instead of after two years, as proposed by the Americans. When it became obvious that the decision would be for the two years, the Creoles, who were interested in manufacturing voters as quickly as possible, favored beginning the waiting period from the time of the immigrant's arrival in New Orleans. The Americans advocated that this period begin after he became a citizen, and it was this plan which was finally adopted. Eustis was sure that the excitement over how long a foreigner must wait before he could vote was caused by party politics and that the party which stood to gain from a shorter waiting period would favor it, but that the party which would lose from such a measure would be against it.[19] His reasoning was later confirmed by fact.

The episode that is most indicative of a Creole-American struggle in New Orleans at the beginning of the 1850's and of the form that party battles would assume in that decade was the fight over how to reunite the city. Climaxing in 1852, the

[18] *Ibid.*, 37–38. [19] *Ibid.*, 93.

conflict shows clearly that the sections had not achieved a harmony of interests. Two different methods of unification were proposed. In the end the Creoles were highly dissatisfied with the plan of reunion, and it was natural that they should seek means to alleviate their distress.

New Orleans from 1836 to 1852 was a divided city. By 1836 the antagonism between the Creoles and Americans had reached such heights that it was decided that separation was the best solution, and the state legislature divided the city into three separate governing bodies called municipalities. The first contained the Creoles of the French Quarter. Its boundaries were the river, Canal Street, and Esplanade Avenue. The second municipality was the American sector, bounded by the river, Canal Street, and Felicity Road. The third municipality was enclosed by the river, Esplanade Avenue, and Chef Menteur. In this district lived many of the Irish and German immigrants who came to New Orleans in the 1840's, although there were many Creoles present also.[20] The city as a whole had a mayor and a common council which regulated general city matters such as wharfage fees and relief to the poor. Each municipality governed itself, including its fiscal affairs, through its own council, with a recorder who served as president. Even such important matters as the police were divided, and each municipality maintained its own force, to the complaint of many citizens who said that offenders fled from one municipality to the other in order to escape arrest.[21]

As long as the business of each municipality was administered entirely by its own council, the division of the city along Creole-American party lines was almost indiscernible. The conflict did appear whenever there was an election of an official to serve the whole city. It is clear, for example, in the 1849 election for sheriff, a powerful local officer. There were two contestants: James Freret, an American, ran on the Whig ticket; and John L. Lewis, who was identified with the Creoles

[20] *L'Orleanais*, September 26, 1850. [All newspapers cited herein were published in New Orleans, unless otherwise noted.]
[21] *Daily Crescent*, January 4, April 4, 1850; May 26, 1851.

through long association, ran on the Democratic ticket. Freret carried every precinct in the American (second) municipality by a rather large majority, while the Creole candidate, Lewis, piled up heavy majorities in the first and third. Lewis won the election through a coalition between the first municipality, Creole, and the third, Creole and immigrant.[22]

A similar situation existed in the election of state senators. They, too, were elected on a city-wide basis after 1845. Election returns reveal that certain candidates received heavy votes from the Americans; others drew their main support from the Creoles and immigrants in the first and third municipalities. The Creole-American conflict existed in New Orleans politics during the period of separation, although it did not become an important factor until later in the 1850's, after consolidation had been accomplished and the municipalities could no longer control their affairs through their own councils.

The period immediately following division of the city in 1836 was marked by advancement throughout the entire city. The municipalities competed with each other for public improvements. Progress was seen in the erection of the Merchants' Exchange, the St. Charles Hotel, the St. Louis Hotel, many banks, the New Basin canal, and a new city hall for the second municipality. But separation did not solve the problems of the city, for as the years wore on the conditions in the first (Creole) and third (immigrant-Creole) municipalities did not continue to improve.

Especially did the financial problem become acute in these districts.[23] From the first of June, 1836, until the thirty-first of December, 1848, the yearly average of the receipts of the third municipality had been $143,185.18. For more than thirteen years the annual deficit had been $63,555.56.[24] In all municipalities there was confusion of administration; the common

[22]*Ibid.*, November 8, 1849.

[23]Reinders, "Social History of New Orleans," I, 115–18. This is an entirely economic interpretation of consolidation. Although basically correct, it overlooks the sectional differences which played so large a part in the question of reunification.

[24]*Daily Crescent,* January 22, 1850.

council went for months without meeting, and police protection was extremely poor in all municipalities. Even the highly esteemed fire-fighting establishment of the city became inadequate. When the St. Charles Hotel burned in January, 1851, the firemen were highly praised for their efforts, but the organization and equipment of the department was criticized in the local press.[25]

With the worsening of financial conditions in the first and third municipalities came increasing antagonism between the Americans and the Creoles. To the Americans it was simply lack of initiative among the citizens of the other municipalities which had caused these conditions. The Americans said that the French of the first municipality were interested only in making money and then returning to France. They complained that the many Spaniards of the third municipality were content to leave things as they were. The go-ahead spirit of the Americans "jars on their national habits. They were very glad to be rid of us—and we are quite willing to continue separated from them." The press of the second (American) municipality often made disparaging remarks about the lack of business in the first and third municipalities or sarcastic comments to the effect that there were not even any vagrants or rascals in these districts, so destitute of activity were they.[26]

Even the press of the third municipality recognized disunity as a leading factor in the lack of prosperity in the city. The *Daily Orleanian*, published also as *L'Orleanais* in French in the third municipality, commented on more than one occasion that the poor state of affairs in the first and third was due to the lack of unity between these two and the American sector. The editor wanted the French groups to amalgamate with the rest, to get an American education in preference to a French, and to learn English. The paper said that the most important barrier between the two sections of the city was language. Division of the two cultures caused suffering to the poor in the midst of the prosperity of the rich. It hoped that the coming

[25] *Daily True Delta*, January 19, 1851.
[26] *Daily Crescent*, April 8, September 24, 1850.

together of the two people could be accomplished in pleasurable as well as business pursuits. Common balls, soirées, and spectacles might promote this spirit of togetherness. Better communication between the second and third municipalities would also bring about greater unity.[27]

The *Daily Delta*, a paper published in the American district but always Creole in sympathy, commented that the St. Charles Hotel fire might have a good effect on New Orleans if it would diffuse the wealth of the city, for the St. Louis, the hotel in the Creole district, had not been rented for two years simply because it was not fashionable for Americans to stay in the lower part of the city. After the fire the management of the St. Charles rented the St. Louis Hotel in order to handle its guests; hence, the occasion for the article. The *Delta* commented that the division of the city in 1836 had been made strictly on appeal to nationalities and had been ruinous to the first and third municipalities. The moving of the Americans into the St. Louis Hotel, however, proved to be a mixed blessing, for in the municipal elections of April, 1851, there was much illegal voting in the precinct of the hotel. The Americans who formerly resided in the St. Charles Hotel now voted in the precinct of the St. Louis, thus creating an American vote in this Creole district.[28]

The lower sections of New Orleans were undoubtedly in a critical condition, but the Americans had little sympathy for their plight, for it was of their own making. Furthermore, the Americans frowned on the peculiarities of the lower sections and decried certain practices there, such as the licensing of masked balls. The *Daily Crescent*, the most outspoken American newspaper, described this as the condoning of "a filthy stew" and hoped that it would be discontinued, for "if vice cannot be altogether suppressed, at least, it will not be allowed to flaunt in gala dress."[29]

Condemnation of the Roman Catholic church appeared in

[27]*L'Orleanais*, September 26, October 9, 18, 1850.
[28]*Daily Delta*, January 21, April 11, 1851.
[29]*Daily Crescent*, March 15, 1851.

the American press from time to time. The revenues of the Roman Catholic church were said to exceed in value the sum of the whole landed estate in the papal dominion. What wonder was it that the people were "so poor, so ignorant, so superstitious."[30] Words such as these did not further the cause of unity among the three districts of New Orleans.

By 1850 the condition of the municipal governments had generally disheartened the people. They complained of wretched streets, of a lack of free water, lights, public improvements, and enterprises that fostered commerce and increased trade. Many businessmen became alarmed. A city, two thirds of which was nearly bankrupt, could repudiate bonds, thereby causing heavy financial losses. This would bring increased taxes, which would not be conducive to new business. Maintaining a three-municipality form of government was another added expense to the already overburdened taxpayer.[31]

Thus public opinion, the hopeless situation of finances, and the pressure of businessmen combined to force a reconsideration of the step taken in 1836. In March of 1850 the New Orleans representatives to the state legislature proposed a charter to reconsolidate the three municipalities, but the legislature refused to take any positive action until the matter was made the issue of a city plebiscite.[32] This was done on April 8, 1850, when the proposal was defeated because of the strong opposition of the second municipality. But A. D. Crossman, successful candidate for mayor on a proconsolidation platform, was favored by all of the municipalities two weeks after the plebiscite. This showed that New Orleans wanted consolidation.[33] The reason for the negative vote lay in the kind proposed. The charter outlined in the plebiscite would have made the three municipalities into three districts; by this plan the Creoles and

[30] *Ibid.*, February 6, 1851.

[31] *Ibid.*, January 31, 1852; Harry Howard Evans, "James Robb, Banker and Pioneer Railroad Builder of Ante-Bellum Louisiana," *Louisiana Historical Quarterly*, XXIII (January, 1940), 177.

[32] John S. Kendall, *History of New Orleans* (Chicago, 1922), I, 172.

[33] *Daily Picayune*, April 25, 1850.

the immigrants would have outvoted the Americans in the unified city council.[34] This would have given the first and third municipalities control over the liquidation of the city debt and would have placed the richest section of the city in a subordinate position.

The Creoles and foreigners endorsed the plan, but the Americans would have none of it. "A few more years will enable the people of the Upper Faubourg to control";[35] then they would think about it, remarked the *Daily Crescent.* The *Daily Delta,* pro-Creole organ, said that it thought the whole city would progress by consolidation. But the *Crescent* answered that the American municipality would not agree to enter into a partnership in which it was recognized as the outstanding member but would have only a minority voice.[36]

The Creoles advanced one argument after another urging consolidation. They were convinced that this move would remedy the financial situation of the nearly bankrupt first and third municipalities by enabling them to use the wealth of the second municipality to their own advantage. This group was sure that $200,000 a year in administrative expenses could be saved by reuniting the city and eliminating two sets of municipal officials.[37] They were positive that more could be obtained from the tax dollar, as nothing was received from the current oppressive taxation except a decent school system and the "exquisite satisfaction of looking at the marble figures which grace the portico of the Municipal Palace, the center of which, being blindfolded, serves as an excellent representative of the conditions of the municipality, when it was persuaded into that piece of extravagance." Where did the tax money go? According to

[34]*Daily Crescent,* March 26, 1850; *Daily Orleanian,* January 30, 1852.

[35]*Daily Crescent,* December 18, 1850.

[36]*Ibid.,* March 1, 1850. Harry Kmen advances the theory that the Sauvé Crevasse of 1849 helped to crystallize opinion in favor of consolidation, but no mention of the Crevasse appears in any of the arguments printed during the campaign of 1852 to unite the city. Harry Kmen, "New Orleans' Forty Days in '49," *Louisiana Historical Quarterly,* XL (January, 1957), 44–45.

[37]*Daily Crescent,* February 16, March 4, 1850.

the Creoles, it went to support three extravagant municipal governments, and three sets of offices where only one was needed.[38]

The Creoles maintained that, besides improving the financial condition of the city, consolidation would provide for greater efficiency in other aspects of the city administration. A unified police force would prevent offenders from fleeing from one municipality to another in an effort to escape justice.[39] Fire protection would be increased, and transportation facilities improved. It was hoped that a heightened efficiency in city government would cause a rise in the price of real estate.[40]

American opposition to the Creoles' plan of consolidation was based primarily on one issue—economics. As the Americans put it, since the second municipality bonds were at par, they could see no reason to inflict the debts of the other two municipalities upon themselves. Each municipality should pay its own way. The American section would not accept any plan which might jeopardize its leadership of the commercial prosperity fostered during the period of independent control. It was beyond reason to submit to a reunion which entailed shouldering that portion of the city debt which the other divisions had incurred and were unable to pay.[41] Under such an arrangement the first and third municipalities would simply sit back and enjoy the profits of American business acumen. Further, as the Americans expressed it, consolidation would not do away with national prejudice, perhaps because they as well as the Creoles did not wish to do away with it. From late 1849 until early 1851 the arguments ran in the foregoing manner. The Creole and immigrant districts pressed as hard as they could to secure consolidation of the city; the Americans rejected union on the grounds that they would lose their autonomy.

[38]*Daily Delta,* December 17, 1850.
[39]*Louisiana Courier,* April 3, 1850.
[40]*Daily Delta,* October 23, 1850.
[41]*Daily Crescent,* March 4, 1850.

In April of 1851 the city council of Lafayette, a small town adjoining New Orleans at Felicity Street, proposed annexation of their community to New Orleans.[42] Final action on the matter was taken on December 17 of the same year when the Lafayette council passed the following resolution:

> Whereas, The four Municipal governments embraced by the cities of New Orleans and Lafayette have the most intimate possible union, in interest, in purpose, in territory, and in destiny and should, therefore, be united in feeling and spirit, irrespective of the arbitrary lines indicated by Felicity Road, Canal street and Esplanade street, which tend to array one portion of this community against the other; therefore, be it
>
> *Resolved*, That the distracted, sectional and overwhelmingly expensive system of government prevailing in the community, is wholly unworthy longer of a people now aroused to the importance of reform and public improvement.
>
> *Resolved*, That the consolidation of the four governments will give rise to no antagonism of feeling or interests between the two extremities of the city; but, on the contrary, will promote that spirit of compromise and unity of feeling which must necessarily result from similar location and relations to the centre of the city.
>
> *Resolved*, That the consolidation of the city of Lafayette with the city of New Orleans, now about to consolidate her three Municipalities, is with the people of Lafayette, as well as with the people of New Orleans, both in a commercial and financial point of view, a simple measure of self-protection and preservation; and that it is now resolved upon by the people of this city with great nuanimity [*sic*].[43]

[42]*Daily Delta*, April 11, 1851.

[43]*Daily Crescent*, December 27, 1851, quoting the Lafayette *Louisiana State Republican*, December 26, 1851; Kathryn C. Briede, "A History of the City of Lafayette" (unpublished master's thesis, Tulane University, 1937), 91.

Ten days later that city voted overwhelmingly in favor of consolidation.[44]

This new plan was exactly what the Americans needed, and they immediately took up the cry for consolidation of New Orleans and annexation of Lafayette. Without it the Americans were compressed between Felicity and Canal streets. Unless an area for expansion were made available to the second municipality, consolidation spelled ultimate political oblivion for the Americans. Both the American section and Lafayette were satisfied, but the proposal to include this community was by no means unanimously accepted by the people of New Orleans; the Creoles fought it to the end. This Creole opposition brought forth a startling announcement from Lafayette to the effect that, if she should be excluded from the consolidation, all of her harbor dues would be abolished, and vessels could use her magnificent wharf without charge. The unionists claimed that this development would mean ruin for the port of New Orleans.

These views were aired in the charged language of the *Daily Crescent,* which supported the American plan of consolidation: "If Lafayette do this, the injury to New Orleans will be incalculable. It will ruin the Third Municipality; it will prostrate the First; it will shatter the Second; it will take all the shipping and boats up into Lafayette, and with them, a large portion of our trade; it will make Lafayette what the Second Municipality now is. Boats and ships are not going to pay $100 or $200 for what can be had for nothing. . . . Consolidation without Lafayette will, bringing disaster to New Orleans, injure the whole State, and set back every plan of Internal Improvement for twenty years."[45] This was blackmail on the part of Lafayette or propaganda manufactured by the Americans, since Lafayette would hardly have been willing to forego the revenue of her wharf.

The plan to unite the adjacent town with the rest of the city reversed the roles of the Americans and Creoles, for the Americans now championed this new form of consolidation,

[44] *Daily Crescent,* January 8, 1852. [45] *Ibid.,* February 2, 1852.

and the Creoles bitterly opposed it. The *Daily Crescent* sarcastically asked for an explanation for this about-face on the part of the first and third municipalities. The Americans used economic arguments, as usual. The second municipality held $40,000,000 in taxable property; the first, $20,000,000; and the third, $10,000,000. This meant that the second municipality had $10,000,000 more taxable property than the first and third combined. Why, the Americans demanded, should the second municipality be forced to assume a large proportion of the debt of her neighbors and share "in a most ruinous decree of liquidation?"[46] If Lafayette were excluded, the Creoles would control the council and the liquidation of the city debt, and the second municipality would indefinitely remain a minority. These arguments, combined with the prospect of a free port in Lafayette, made consolidation without that city unthinkable, from the American point of view. Under the new plan the Americans could potentially control the council, and each of the municipalities would share in the liquidation of the debt in proportion to their preconsolidation indebtedness.

In opposing the inclusion of Lafayette, the Creoles harped on the argument that such a move might promote "sectional and political feelings."[47] What they really meant was that without Lafayette the first and third municipalities would control the city, but that with Lafayette, the Americans could dominate; this, from their standpoint, would cause sectional and political irritation. When the Americans grew even more determined to include Lafayette, the Creoles then fell back on the argument that the town could not be absorbed because it was located in Jefferson Parish. This contention was quickly turned, however, as it was demonstrated that the parish line could easily be extended, which was subsequently done. Every objection advanced by the Creoles to the inclusion of Lafayette was penetrated and revealed to be a mere rationalization of their desire to maintain a grip on the city administration.

In December of 1851 the *Daily Crescent* announced, "There

[46] *Ibid.*, January 31, February 11, 1852.
[47] *Daily Delta,* December 23, 1851.

is something in this whole attempt to exclude Lafayette from any plan of Consolidation, which to us is curiously inexplicable." In a little over a month the *Crescent* had discovered exactly what that curious, inexplicable item was; in its January 29, 1852, issue it commented on a bill put forth by John Slidell, so it said, which provided for consolidation without Lafayette. This bill would make the second municipality, "the servile treasury—a sold Esau—for the other municipalities."[48] If the bill should pass, said the editor, the second municipality would have been sacrificed, for it would have been forever placed in the minority by two to one. Even the organ of the third municipality publicly announced that such would be the case; in the January 30, 1852, issue it said that the first and third could have preponderance on the board by acting in concert, although it qualified the statement by saying that this would not always be the case.[49] For the Americans the matter was no longer "curiously inexplicable."

By the first week in February, two weeks before the final passage of the bill by the state legislature, the word "consolidation" was on every tongue. Said the *Daily Crescent:*

> Consolidation. This word is now frequently heard as an oath on our streets. The draymen use it in quarreling on the Levee, and the Aldermen use it in squabbling in the Council chambers. Our Legislators in Baton Rouge go into hysterics over it, and our newspapers talk about nothing else but that and Kossuth. We were yesterday informed in the First Municipality that the good people of that patriotic and faithful district are all becoming insane, and we witnessed one terrible fight that was got up by the force of the word. One of the combatants caught the thumb of a police officer in his teeth, and came near making a case of separation of the matter. We believe that ninety-nine out of every hundred of our citizens are in favor of Consolidation, and that three out of four are in favor of the annexation of Lafayette. Hur-

[48] *Daily Crescent*, December 30, 1851, January 13, 29, 1852.
[49] *Daily Orleanian*, January 30, 1852.

rah for the annexation of Texas, Cuba, Kossuth, and Lafayette!"[50]

The tone of the article clearly indicated confidence in the passage of the bill.

This confidence was justified. On the next day, February 6, James Robb, an influential American financier and member of the state legislature who was supposedly against the inclusion of Lafayette, announced that he was in favor of it and would do all in his power to insure its success.[51] Since to include it in the same bill with the consolidation of New Orleans might have endangered the whole plan, Lafayette was united by a supplementary bill. About two days before the issue came to a vote, a large delegation from the second municipal council went to Baton Rouge to lobby for the inclusion of Lafayette. Evidently they were successful, for final passage in the state legislature came on February 13, 1852, by a vote of seventy-six to six. On February 24 Governor James Walker signed both bills, and the three municipalities of New Orleans, together with the city of Lafayette, became one, though the first and third municipalities protested the inclusion of the outside community until the very end.[52]

After consolidation the municipalities were known as districts. Two of them changed numbers; the second (American) municipality became the first district; the first (Creole) municipality became the second district. The third municipality became the third district. Newly annexed Lafayette was a new district, the fourth.

The opening of the decade of the 1850's found New Orleans engaged in a struggle which, although disguised, was essentially an extension of the battle between Creoles and Americans for control of the city. The outcome of this contest was a victory for the Americans, for it was their plan of consolidation which

[50]*Daily Crescent*, February 6, 1852.

[51]Earlier rumors had circulated that Robb opposed the inclusion of Lafayette because he had speculated in third municipality bonds and would therefore favor a consolidation which would do the most for these bonds. *Daily Crescent*, January 29, 31, February 2, 1852.

[52]*Ibid.*, February 6, 10, 11, 12, 13, 25, 1852.

was finally enacted into law. But the unity that emerged from the act of 1852 was purely physical; emotionally the city remained separated. The Creoles had governed New Orleans before the split of 1836. After the division they governed their own section. It is not logical to assume that these Creoles, masters of New Orleans since it was founded, in 1852 suddenly realized that their power was gone and gracefully bowed out to the Americans. Such was not their nature. They fought back. But the Americans would enter no partnership involving the loss of control of their section. Ever increasing in numbers and wealth, they were just as determined that they should rule. This is the setting for the career of the Know Nothing party in New Orleans.

CHAPTER TWO

# *Metamorphosis*

THE changes produced by the consolidation of the municipalities in 1852 colored municipal, state, and federal politics in New Orleans for the next ten years. Two developments altered the structure of city politics. First, the political party became the dominant factor in municipal elections. Second, consolidation reopened the Creole-American conflict which had more or less lain dormant since the division of New Orleans in 1836. These two consequences made possible the rise and continuance of the Know Nothing party until the fall of the city in 1862.

Aspirants to public office in New Orleans had previously been nominated largely on the basis of personal accomplishment, with little regard to party affiliation. It was said that party names were not even mentioned in the city council until as late as 1846.[1] None the less, as early as 1842 the Democratic party successfully ran Denis Prieur as its candidate for mayor. The Whigs, however, gave their name to no candidate for city office until 1844; then they did so by means of a primary rather than by the usual party caucus used by the Democrats. As late as 1848 a Whig candidate for mayor, A. D. Crossman, was elected with the aid of many Democratic votes, giving proof that a man's personal influence still exerted as much power as party affiliation.[2] The mid-1840's marked the end of nonparty nominations, but the Whig press continued to support the idea until 1852 when the city was consolidated and conditions in New Orleans forced a change in practice. At

[1] *Daily Crescent,* April 4, 1851.
[2] Kendall, *History of New Orleans,* I, 162, 165.

that time fluidity of votes between the two parties was no longer possible because of the new alignment by which each section of the city was identified with a particular party. Political parties became firmly entrenched in municipal politics until the Civil War. Judah P. Benjamin summed up the importance of party allegiance in municipal politics in 1852 when he declared that a vote for the Whigs in that year's city election would mean a vote for the Whigs in the national elections several months later.[3]

The crystallizing of party politics was a phenomenon common to many American cities of the time, but the Creole-American clash was unique to New Orleans. The flame of this conflict was fanned to new heights during the years immediately following consolidation, only to be extinguished within a decade. Just as consolidation masked the struggle from 1850 to 1852, so party politics concealed it for the next ten years. This is not to say that party politics would not have appeared had there been no Creole-American conflict, for party contests had already arisen in the municipal council. But the evidence indicates that the cultural hostility between the two groups added greatly to the bitterness of the political fray.

Prior to consolidation the relationship of the three municipal councils to the common council of the city was somewhat similar to that between the states and the federal government; except for powers specifically given to the central government by the city charter each municipality was autonomous and therefore had no fear of being dominated by its neighbors in internal matters. In a single, united council, however, the first and third municipalities (Creole and immigrant) planned after unification to take advantage of their superior numbers to control the city. This was not a postconsolidation development; it was in existence in the general council while the city was still separated. In June of 1851, for example, the first and third had combined to outvote the second in reducing the

[3]Pierce Butler, *Judah P. Benjamin* (Philadelphia, 1907), 103; *Commercial Bulletin*, February 18, 1852.

wharfage rates in their municipalities. "We have not the least objections," one American editor caustically wrote, "to the Third Municipality legislating for the Second, as in fact in the present instance they have done; but we claim the right of being consulted."[4] Mayor Crossman rejected the bill, but it was passed over his veto.[5]

As long as the municipalities remained autonomous, there was no occasion for any of them to throw its entire support to a particular party, since competing parties could exist within the same municipality without threatening its self-government. In the election of 1850 the Whigs were victorious in the first and second municipalities, while the third went Democratic in line with tradition in that district.[6] After the consolidation bill passed the state legislature, the situation changed. Pressure for political reorganization was apparent throughout the city. It took definite form in the municipal elections of 1852, although a party alignment by municipalities had not yet taken place. Yet it must have been obvious that the lower section of the city would coalesce within the Democratic party in order to dominate the municipal government. Also, the second municipality was not yet numerically superior to the other two municipalities combined, as the arguments during the consolidation struggle indicated. Given these two circumstances, the Americans decided that their best interests lay in promoting two definite parties at the municipal level. In this way the first district (American) could at least attain a proper voice in party councils in order to receive its just share of representation in municipal councils. For this reason the Americans tried to make prosperity the keynote of political contests and insisted that such phrases as uptown and downtown be forgotten. Above all, no independent movements should be tolerated, for such would be likely to produce candidates from one particular section to the disadvantage of the outnumbered Americans.

The American press, therefore, urged the parties to make

[4] *Commercial Bulletin*, June 24, 1851.
[5] *Daily Crescent*, June 24, 1851.
[6] *Daily Picayune*, April 25, 1850.

nominations for the principal city offices. Demagogues then could not make sectional appeals, urging that this or that man be voted for because he came from this or that municipality, and thus defeat the whole object of consolidation. "If parties nominate, the candidates and their friends would as soon handle live coals as make sectional appeals." In other words, if nominations were made on an independent basis, the American interests might well be outvoted by those below Canal Street. The *Daily Crescent*, an American newspaper, actually said that, if parties should make the nominations, they would have to be divided throughout the different portions of the city; but if the candidates should run as independents, those successful might come predominantly from one part of the city. This could lead to the outbreak of sectional feeling again. Another advantage in supporting one of the two major political parties was that New Orleans could thereby continue to guide the rest of Louisiana in national politics. The *Crescent* explained that whichever party carried New Orleans usually carried the rest of Louisiana. This was in part an argument of expediency; it was seldom true. An additional reason for nominating by party was to prevent a "scrub race," wherein five or six men might run for the same office and by so doing help elect the least deserving.

Judged by their appeals throughout the campaign, the Americans felt most at home in the Whig party. They often called on the Whigs to stick by their party to a man and not to swap votes as had been the case in other elections. A Whig victory was imperative. They noted that General John L. Lewis, the Democratic candidate for mayor in 1852 and thoroughly identified with the Creoles, planned to march his militia brigade up into the first district (American section). Such a move was unprecedented and significant.[7]

The most important reason for the election of a Whig mayor was his control over the election machinery. Because of the

[7]*Daily Crescent*, February 16, 17, 19, 1852; *Commercial Bulletin*, February 17, 18, 27, 28, March 16, 17, 18, 1852.

immense appointing power given to that officer by the new consolidation charter, he could fill with members of his own party all of the posts of commissioners of elections. These commissioners decided who was properly qualified to vote. Present at the polls throughout election day, they virtually determined the electorate. The power to assign such key officials could be a "tremendous engine" in the hands of the successful candidate. It gave the mayor inordinate power in the selection of city, state, and federal officials. If such power went to an independent, which the Americans took to mean a person from the lower part of the city, uptown New Orleans would suffer.[8]

The development which the American Whigs most feared came to pass in March, 1852, when an independent movement appeared. For the mayoralty there were only two candidates, the Whig A. D. Crossman and the Democrat John L. Lewis. But for all the lesser executive offices and for the board and assistant board of aldermen there were three sets of candidates—Whig, Democratic, and Independent. The "ostensible" purpose of the movement was to elect an independent ticket, but this was impossible. The Whigs recognized it as a plot contrived by the Democrats to split their party.[9]

Supposedly composed of Whigs and Democrats, the Independent Reform movement proposed to free the city from the "baleful influence" of party politics. To this the Americans asked, "Has the millenium been reached? Is the 'lamb and lion laying [*sic*] down together'? Or has the lion yet been seen 'eating straw like the ox'? When these things shall have happened, (if in our day,) then these gentlemen, who have sat themselves up as workers of wonders, may consummate their desires."

That only the *Daily Delta* and the *Daily True Delta* supported the Independent movement was further proof that it was really Democratic-inspired. The editors of both of these

[8] *Daily Crescent*, February 28, 1852.
[9] *Ibid.*, March 12, 16, 1852; *Commercial Bulletin*, March 17, 1852.

papers were known to be leaders of the Democratic party who wished more than all else to see the destruction of the Whig party.[10] The Americans cited as evidence the stand taken by the *Daily Delta* on the Whig candidacy of W. H. Garland, a popular citizen of the first, or American, district. The *Daily Delta* labeled the whole Whig ticket the "Garland ticket." The effect of the quotation marks was to make the title appear to mean that the Democratic press had copied this from a Whig journal. It was an attempt to make the Whig party look as if it were a machine in the hands of one person, and this person a resident of the American section–the first district. The intent was clearly to discourage the lower section of the city from voting for such a candidate or ticket.[11] The Americans were sure that the strategy was designed to discredit the Whig candidates one by one and so destroy the ticket's effectiveness. They could see no good at all in the Independents. "We are to have three sets of candidates, instead of two; with the effect that we see around us, of hotter conflicts, angrier collisions, and more rancor and bitterness than we remember for many a day in one of the regular contests of whigs and democrats."[12]

The Whigs succeeded in electing a mayor and all the officers in the executive department of the city government. They also managed to eke out a bare majority in the council, but many of the Independent candidates were victorious. The municipal election of 1852 demonstrated the trend toward party alignment. The greatest Whig strength was in the first district (the American section, formerly the second municipality), while the Independent strength lay in the second (formerly the first municipality) and third, the Creole and foreign districts. Although many of the Creoles still voted the Whig ticket, in the Creole and immigrant sections many Independents were elected to the council.[13] The Whigs accused them of being Democrats in disguise; these accusations proved true, as the

[10]*Commercial Bulletin,* March 17, 1852; *Bee,* March 12, 20, 1852; *Daily Crescent,* March 12, 19, May 24, 1852.

[11]*Daily Crescent,* March 13, 1852, *Daily Delta,* March 12, 1852.

[12]*Daily Crescent,* March 13, 17, 1852.

[13]*Daily Picayune,* March 24, 1852.

Independents consistently voted with the Democrats in the council.[14] When the newspapers supporting the Independents at the time of the election later switched their support to the Democrats, Whig opinion was further substantiated.

In this election many former Democrats of the first (American) district apparently voted Whig, while many erstwhile Whigs in the second (Creole) district converted to the Democratic party. The reason for these shifts is not difficult to understand. If the Americans could at this time, when they were not yet preponderant in numbers, throw their united support behind the Whigs, they could hope to gain much greater influence in party councils. More and more Americans felt the need of a political hierarchy controlled by themselves. The Creoles turned to the Democratic party in order to make the coalition with the Democratic third district effective. If these two, the second and third districts, could present a united front, they could then dominate municipal and possibly even state and national politics in New Orleans.

The trend toward party alignment was strongly reflected in the campaign when the Democrats attempted to make it appear that the Whigs had been against consolidation. The Whigs pointed out that the real issue had been the kind of consolidation and accused the Democrats of favoring the wrong form of reunion—one which did not include Lafayette.[15] The Americans stood for consolidation only if it included Lafayette, while the Creoles and immigrants of the third district staunchly opposed the inclusion of Lafayette. The Whigs, therefore, became mainly the party of the Americans, and the Democrats mainly the party of the Creoles and immigrants. At the time of the struggle the manner of consolidation was purely a sectional matter and nonparty, but by the municipal election of 1852 the union had become a party as well as a sectional issue, another strong indication of the alignment which was taking place.

The results of this election were by no means an unqualified

[14] *Bee*, March 12, 1852; *Daily Crescent*, May 24, 26, 1852.
[15] *Daily Crescent*, March 3, April 21, 1852.

American victory, for the Whigs were not exclusively Americans. Controller Ovide DeBuys and Surveyor S. Pilié were both prominent Creoles. A. D. Crossman, candidate for mayor, while not a Creole, was an American merchant who came to New Orleans shortly after the Louisiana Purchase and who had the confidence of the whole city, including the Creoles. W. H. Garland was the only candidate for executive office who was a thorough-going American. But at least the election was a victory for that party in which the American interests were best represented. The results of this election indicate only a trend, not an accomplished fact. Within the next two years the Creole and immigrant districts (second and third) were to perfect their coalition. Then the Americans would determine that this coalition must be defeated; party alignment by district would be completed; and the Know Nothing party, successor to the Whigs, would be there to battle against the Creoles and immigrants.

After the municipal elections of March, 1852, the next major political canvass in New Orleans was the presidential campaign of the same year. From the opening of the campaign the outlook was bleak for New Orleans Whigs. The nomination of Winfield Scott chagrined them. "We confess that this nomination has greatly disappointed us. Even now, we feel stunned and dizzy in disappointed hopes. . . . Our pen lags in its wonted duty."[16] Slavery was the only real issue of the campaign, and both parties were of the southern point of view. This meant no heated contest could be sitrred up over platforms. Further, of greater interest to New Orleans Whigs was the ratification of the state constitution drawn up by them in 1852. It was to be voted on in the presidential election.

Ratification was imperative. Not only were there economic provisions necessary to their interests, but also it was thought that Whig power might be perpetuated in Louisiana through the method of representation written into the new state law. Henceforth, apportionment to the legislature would be based on the total number of whites and blacks. This gave the slave-

[16] *Ibid.*, June 24, 1852; *Commercial Bulletin*, June 23, 1852.

holding Whig parishes a majority in the state legislature which they otherwise would not have had. It was a coalition between the wealthy Whigs of New Orleans and the wealthy Whig slave owners.

Because the new constitution was more important to the New Orleans Whigs than the presidential campaign, many who voted that November for the constitution did not cast a ballot for the president. It was even rumored that many Whigs swapped a vote for the Democratic presidential candidate in return for the Democrat's support of the Whig constitution.[17]

The city gave Democrat Franklin Pierce a majority of about 150 votes. The third (immigrant) district and the fourth (Lafayette) gave him majorities of well over a hundred each.[18] The second (Creole) district was almost equally divided between the two candidates; and the first (American) went for Scott by 105 ballots.[19] The trend toward party alignment by district, initiated in municipal politics, did not show up in the presidential balloting.

Fewer votes were cast in 1852 than in the 1848 election, although the city had grown considerably each year. This relative decrease was to be continued through 1857 because of the mounting disorderliness at the polls in New Orleans. Increasingly voters stayed at home rather than risk the affrays that were growing more common with each election. The Whigs, of course, blamed this on the immigrants, and the disfranchisement of many people by this means was one of the reasons for the growth and development of the Know Nothing party.

Within the smaller total vote there was a relative decrease in the Whig vote in every district in the city. Only slight was

[17]Merlin Elaine Owen, "The Presidential Elections of 1852, 1856, and 1860 in New Orleans" (unpublished master's thesis, Tulane University, 1957), 31, 34.

[18]It was not until later in the decade that enough Americans moved into Lafayette to counteract the large number of Irish and German immigrants who were settling there.

[19]Owen, "Presidential Elections," 41.

the change in the Creole district, which had generally been almost evenly divided in preceding presidential elections. But the downward trend was pronounced in the Irish-German immigrant area, the third district. Before 1845 the third was inhabited largely by Creoles who spilled over from the second area. With the great increase in German and Irish immigration after the Irish potato famine in 1846 and the revolutions in Germany in 1848, many of the immigrants moved into the third district and later into the "Irish channel" above the city.[20] With the increased numbers of immigrants in these districts, the vote shifted from Whig to Democrat by a heavy majority. In the 1852 presidential election this shifting was very important, for the vote of the third district together with that of the fourth, Lafayette, built a majority of over two hundred for Pierce, a majority which could not be offset by Scott's advantage in the American section.

More significant was the change that took place in the American district, which cast about 50 per cent of the city's vote. It had been heavily and consistently Whig in every presidential campaign since 1836, yet in 1852 Scott carried the district by only 105 votes. Previously, the Whig strength in the American section had been large enough to offset the Democratic vote in the other sections of the city. This sharp decline of the Whig vote in the American section in 1852 gave Pierce the victory in New Orleans. In the effort to get their constitution adopted the Whigs neglected to canvass sufficiently for their party's presidential nominee. Vote swapping also contributed to the decreased Whig numbers.

The importance of this shift appears in high relief when the district votes on the state constitution are considered. The Irish-German district (third) voted against the Whig constitution by a vote of 885 to 745. The Creole district (second) gave it a small majority of 1,597 to 1,299, and Lafayette did the same—670 to 519. But the American section, the stronghold

[20]The "Irish channel" was a section in the fourth district bounded by Felicity Street, Magazine Street, Toledano Street, and the Mississippi River, in which many Irish immigrants settled.

of the Whigs, went overwhelmingly for the constitution with a vote of 2,730 to 1,158.[21] New Orleans as a whole voted for the Whig constitution but against the Whig presidential candidate. Since slavery was the chief issue of the presidential campaign of 1852, apparently many New Orleans Whigs felt that the institution was safer with the Democrats. To local Whigs the economic issues were all-important; they threw their support solidly behind ratification of the new state constitution.

Many New Orleans Whigs disliked their party's platform, because it was a lukewarm southern victory in that the Compromise of 1850 was accepted only until "time and experience shall demonstrate the necessity of further legislation to guard against the evasion of the laws on the one hand and the abuse of their powers on the other."[22] Also, it was thought that Scott represented the radical Seward abolitionist wing of the Whig party, in spite of the general's loud endorsement of the Compromise. Faced with Scott on the one hand and the Democrats on the other, many of the New Orleans Whigs simply did not vote. Thus, a large increase in the Democratic vote, an increase in the number of immigrants in Lafayette and the third district, and a significant decrease in the vote of the dominant Whig stronghold of New Orleans, the American section, gave the city to Franklin Pierce.

Despite growing internal troubles in the Louisiana Democratic party, it presented a front united enough to rout the Whigs in New Orleans in the December, 1852, state elections. The Democratic party showed its Creole colors by nominating for senators John L. Lewis, who was thoroughly associated with the Creoles, and Alexander Davis from the second district, who was "one of the most popular of our Creole citizens." At least half of the candidates were Creole in sympathy.[23]

Although the Democrats won all offices, analysis of the returns by districts emphasizes the position of the Americans. In the first (American) district the majorities for the Demo-

[21]Owen, "Presidential Elections," 41–44.
[22]*Ibid.*, 24.
[23]*Weekly Delta*, December 12, 1852.

cratic candidates were barely one hundred each, while in the second (Creole) district all Democrats won by a majority of at least three hundred to four hundred votes. In the third district the results were even more striking, for there the vote was at least two to one in favor of the Democrats.[24] Thus, the coalition between the second and third (Creole and immigrant) districts was accomplished by this election. Within a year the situation would demand drastic action.

Between 1852 and 1856 the Whigs disintegrated as a national party. With the disappearance of the organization which most represented American interests in New Orleans, it was absolutely necessary for that group to find another party, since municipal as well as state and federal politics were now organized on such a basis. While most Southern Whigs were generally finding a niche somewhere in the Democratic party, this was impossible for New Orleans Americans. Locally, by 1852, the Democratic party was enough identified with the Creoles and immigrants to keep the Americans out. The election itself represents another step in this process of identification and is therefore significant as one of the events that forced the Americans into the Know Nothing party.

[24]*Daily Crescent*, December 29, 1852.

CHAPTER THREE

# The Beginnings of Sam[1]

THE high-water mark for the Democratic party in New Orleans came in 1853. The sectional conflict, reopened during the consolidation struggle, caused the second (Creole) and the third (Creole-immigrant) districts to join forces under the Democratic banner. For nearly two years the coalition worked, effectively overriding the Americans.

In the aldermanic elections of 1853 the Democrats of the second and third districts sufficiently organized to gain complete control of the city council. In this off-year contest they elected seven aldermen and twenty-one assistant aldermen. The Whig press looked forward with fear and trembling; events proved their foreboding justified.[2]

The new council was quick to press its advantage over the American Whig mayor. Members of the Democratic party in the city influenced fellow Democrats in the state legislature to amend the city charter of 1852, which gave to the mayor complete authority over the police force. According to the amendments this responsibility was now vested in a police board composed of the mayor and the four recorders, each with one vote. The Democrats controlled the five-man board, since it contained only two Whigs—the mayor, and the recorder of the fourth district.[3]

[1]"Sam" was the symbol used by the Know Nothing party in all of its campaigns. Whenever Know Nothings appeared in great numbers at political rallies or during elections, "Sam" was said to have appeared.

[2]*Daily Crescent*, March 29, 1853.

[3]*Ibid.*, November 1, 1853. This was the last time the first (American) district had a Democratic recorder.

Repercussions from the act were most strongly felt a year later in the municipal elections of 1854. The board then comprised four Democrats and one Whig, Recorder H. M. Summers from the first district. Summers was completely stymied, even to the point of not being able to choose the policemen for his district, as was the custom. He resigned in protest, and the council appointed a Democrat, George Y. Bright, to take his place. The result was the emergence of a Democratic police force, a valuable asset to that party at election time.[4]

Again working through the state legislature, the Democrats tightened their grip in April, 1853, by striking from the city charter the provision which required that a member of the council remain out of office for six months before he could be elected to any other city position. The reason for this move was partisan. Soon there was to be a vacancy in one of the recorderships, and the Democrats had chosen a man to fill it. The stumbling block was the city charter. Despite the opposition of the mayor and his Whig supporters, it was suitably amended and the Democrats elected C. Ramos, a Creole from the second district.

The apex of the Democratic party's attempt to entrench itself as the dominant political power in New Orleans was the proposal in November, 1853, of a so-called health ordinance to establish the position of public health officer for the city. This official was to have been paid $6,000 a year, a salary greater than that of any public servant in the state except the chief justice of the supreme court. His control of patronage through the appointing power would have been greater than that of the governor. The police would have been subject to his requirements, and he was to have complete jurisdiction over the removal of dilapidated buildings and similar projects. His time of office was to last until May of 1856. Positive that this was another attempt by the Democrats to provide a political plum for one of the faithful, the Whigs campaigned vig-

[4]*Ibid.*, April 12, 25, October 11, 15, 1854; *Louisiana Courier*, October 21, 1853.

orously against it.[5] The board of assistant aldermen passed the health ordinance by a vote of eleven to three but decided that it could not become law since it involved an appropriation of more than $1,000. According to the charter, such appropriations required a majority vote of the twenty-six members of the assistant board. When the ordinance was tabled,[6] the Whigs breathed a sigh of relief, for they feared that the Democratic board might go on creating positions until every member had been provided for, to the complete depletion of the city treasury.

Complaints about streets indicated that parties were aligning by districts. Whereas eight months earlier the streets had been clean and orderly, by June of 1853 they were described as festering and filthy, especially between Poydras and Canal, the heart of the American district.[7] The growing deadlock between Whig executive and Democratic council was evident when the Whig controller, James Jolles, was accused of neglect of city sanitation. Jolles insisted that, although his weekly reports to the council showed that the street contractors were doing nothing, the board had taken no action. Instead, the Democratic council had infuriated the American section by laying a plank road on Prytania Street, even though the residents had signed a petition protesting its construction as incommodious and unhealthful. The controller's language was strong to the point of being abusive, and the council considered impeachment. They never took action, however, and he served out his term.[8]

The Americans presented a petition to the council to move the polling places from the "coffee-houses," as many of the

[5]*Daily Crescent,* April 20, November 25, 29, 1853. See the *Louisiana Courier,* November 25 and 29, 1853, for Democratic justification of the measure.

[6]*Daily Crescent,* December 21, 1853. The board and the assistant board of aldermen were comparable to the two houses of Congress. An ordinance passed by one had to be approved by the other before becoming law.

[7]*Ibid.,* June 3, July 1, November 25, 1853.

[8]*Ibid.,* July 21, 22, 23, 1853; *Commercial Bulletin,* July 22, 25, 1853; *Louisiana Courier,* July 23, 1853.

city's saloons were called, to fire stations and school houses. It was met with derision by the Democratic council, who scornfully recommended submitting it to the educational committee. The Whigs retorted angrily that the Democrats were merely afraid of losing the votes of their immigrant political allies.[9]

The New Orleans press clearly reflected the swirl and flow of political currents as the two major parties formed along nationalistic lines. The *Daily Crescent*, published in the first district and traditionally representing American interests, fell in behind the Whigs and, after their demise, behind their successor, the American or Know Nothing party. The *Louisiana Courier* was published in French as well as in English in the second district. Representing the Creoles, it consistently supported the Democrats.[10] Emile LeSere, the owner, was one of the leaders of the Democratic party in the state.[11] The *Daily Orleanian*, also published in French and English, represented primarily the immigrants of the third district. It was generally Democratic in sympathy, but not so strongly partisan as the other two. In these newspapers, which were the organs of expression in the districts in which they were printed, the Democratic position soon became synonymous with the Creole point of view, while the Whig program and later that of the Know Nothings, was identified with American interests.

By 1853 the Americans knew that, even though their numbers were increasing rapidly and the American district was growing apace, they would never be able to catch up with the mounting tide of immigrants from Ireland and Germany who were pouring annually into New Orleans. As these immigrants coalesced politically with the Creoles, the Americans increasingly realized that the control of the city which

[9]*Daily Crescent*, October 31, 1853; *Commercial Bulletin*, October 31, 1853.

[10]*Daily Crescent*, January 7, 1851.

[11]W. Darrell Overdyke, *The Know Nothing Party in the South* (Baton Rouge, 1950), 23.

they had sought by consolidation had slipped away from them. They struck at this coalition by denouncing naturalized citizens and attempting to hinder foreigners from becoming naturalized so that they could vote. Americans warned of the threat of foreign domination of the city; Creoles in reply called upon the immigrants to beware of the Americans.[12] E. J. Carrell, an American candidate for district attorney in 1853, was defeated by the appearance of an anonymous notice accusing him of Creole and foreign sympathies. His public denials were of no avail, and he lost the Whig vote.[13]

Doubtless it was the Creole-foreign alignment which forced the Americans into complete political organization. The Americans had long recognized the infiltration of the local Democratic party by the immigrants, though the influx of foreigners was by no means unique to New Orleans. All of the major American cities, and especially the seaports, were faced with this problem. From the councilmanic elections of 1853 until the outbreak of the Civil War the constant cry of the American press was against the illegal use of the foreign vote by the Democrats, and the whole brunt of American political action was to suppress what they considered an illegal vote. Election statistics after 1852 show that by and large the second (Creole) district turned to the Democratic party in order to use these foreign votes to fight their opponents—the Americans.

The supreme court justice election of April, 1853, offers an excellent example of how the second (Creole) and third (immigrant) districts worked together to defeat the first (American). The candidates were Christian Roselius, a German-born American Whig, and Thomas Slidell, brother of John Slidell, chief of the Democratic party. Through intermarriage and by association the Slidells were both linked with the Creoles. The strategy followed by the Democrats was to accuse Roselius of being nativist in sympathy. The Demo-

[12]*Daily Crescent*, October 26, 1853, March 21, 1854; *Louisiana Courier*, March 22, 1854.

[13]*Daily Crescent*, May 23, 24, 1853.

cratic Creole press stressed this point, while the American press attempted to refute it in editorial after editorial. Speeches of Roselius from the constitutional convention of 1852 were quoted in order to prove that he had been proforeign in his attitudes toward getting the qualifications for voting reduced in order to help the immigrant or naturalized citizen. This was true. Nevertheless, papers like the *Louisiana Courier* constantly pressed the point that Roselius was against all immigrants and that to vote for him was to put a man on the bench who was inimical to their interests. In attempting to counteract this propaganda the *Daily Crescent* stressed the reason Roselius had been such an outstanding lawyer—he was a self-made man and had risen from nothing. Such a man as Thomas Slidell, on the other hand, had been born into affluence and had every opportunity to better himself.[14]

The Democratic strategy was successful and Slidell was elected over Roselius. The results furnish clear evidence that Slidell won because of the Creole-immigrant coalition. In the first (American) district the returns were 1,546 for Slidell and 2,137 for Roselius, who won by a majority of 591. In the second (Creole) district Slidell received 1,569 votes and Roselius 1,246—a majority of 323 for Slidell. In the third (immigrant) district Slidell got 828 votes and Roselius 523—a majority of 305 for Slidell. In the fourth district Slidell led by 18 votes out of a total of 206. Slidell carried the city by 55 votes. The combination of Creoles and immigrants within the Democratic party gave him the victory.

The Whig Americans attributed their loss of the election to two activities by the Democrat Creoles: the purchase of votes and the smearing of Roselius as a nativist. Influenced by this charge against the Whig candidate, immigrant voters had joined with the Creoles to bring victory to the Democratic party.[15]

About six weeks after the supreme court election the *Daily*

[14] *Ibid.*, April 4, 11, 1853; *Commercial Bulletin*, April 4, 1853; *Louisiana Courier*, April 2, 3, 1853.

[15] *Daily Crescent*, April 5, 7, 1853; *Commercial Bulletin*, April 8, 1853.

*Crescent* virtually acknowledged the death of its party. A rumor had been circulating ever since the last presidential election that the Whigs were dying. Firmly denying the charge at first, the editor ended in admitting the disintegration of the party and re-emphasized the virtue of the Whig principles and the need for some new organization. In truth the day of the Whigs was over. The city was virtually abandoned to the Democratic party, in which American interests were so little represented.[16]

The joint strength of the second and third districts increased daily. With the Whig party in pieces, the Americans struck frantically at the coalition's source of power—the mounting tide of immigrants. As the fall election of 1853 for members of the state legislature and parish offices approached, the Americans continued to hammer away at the flagrant and fraudulent use the Democrats were making of the immigrant vote. It was reported that the sixth district court actually had to be closed for a few days in order to bring up the minutes. They were lagging because of the number of applications for naturalization papers, most of them illegal. The Democrats staunchly denied these allegations.[17]

As in the spring municipal elections of 1853, so in the fall, the Creole-immigrant coalition functioned well. The Democrats won all offices elected on a city-wide basis. In the race for sheriff their candidate, Bernard Marigny, beat his Whig opponent, James Freret, by 2,474 votes. In the American district the Whigs had majorities, but these were again offset in the Creole and immigrant sections. In the contest for state representatives, Americans placed some Whig candidates, for they were elected by district. But state senators, chosen on a city-wide basis, were all Democrats, as were the two congressmen elected from the New Orleans area.[18]

Americans were embittered that this election drew the larg-

[16]*Daily Crescent,* May 24, 1853.

[17]*Ibid.,* October 18, 19, 21, 1853; *Louisiana Courier,* October 20, 22, 23, 25, 1853.

[18]*Daily Picayune,* November 9, 1853; *Daily Crescent,* November 10, 1853.

est vote ever cast, despite the depopulation of the city during the recent yellow fever epidemic. Even the noncommittal *Daily Picayune* wryly commented on the increase in an article entitled, "The Growth of New Orleans," contrasting the vote of 9,865 cast in the mayoralty contest of 1852, a very spirited election, with the 12,876 cast in 1853. With biting sarcasm the *Picayune* calculated that at this rate New Orleans would have 700,000 people by April 1, 1862. While the article did not explicitly say so, the implication was strong that the Democrats won by the use of many fraudulent votes.[19]

The most important reason advanced by the Americans to explain the landslide of the Democrats was that the Democrat-controlled municipal council had appointed none but "locofoco Democrats" to be inspectors, and they in turn counted only Democratic votes. Dominating the council was tantamount to controlling elections at the state and national level, and therefore the party in power on the council virtually determined the outcome of these elections.[20]

The year 1853 closed with the Democrats practically in complete control of New Orleans politics at all levels. The Whig party had succeeded in electing only a few members to the state legislature from the first district. The demoralized condition of their party left the Americans in a state of despair. With the electorate almost completely determined by the Democrats and the members of that party largely representative of downtown New Orleans, the uptown portion of the city was becoming politically inarticulate.

To the Americans 1854 was at first but a continuation of the same dismal situation of 1853. A grand jury report showed that many prisoners had not been placed on the court dockets; convicted lawbreakers either were not put in jail or were released from charges that were not bailable. In some cases bonds had been accepted when the security was known to be no good. The weak registration law, recently passed by the

[19]*Daily Picayune,* November 11, 1853.

[20]*Daily Crescent,* November 8, 11, 1853; *Louisiana Courier,* November 11, 1853.

legislature, was almost worthless since noncompliance was not a bar to voting. Naturalization frauds continued daily. According to the Americans the Irish were organized into bands by the Democrats and marched to the polls to vote, where hand-picked Irish Democratic inspectors and election officials permitted them to vote without question. Plural voting was rampant, and the protest of the citizenry had no effect.[21] At the bottom of the Americans' inability to gain a fair share in the voice of government was this use by the Democrats of the ever-mounting foreign or immigrant vote.

With the demise of the Whig party nationally[22] its anti-immigrant elements found outlet in a revival of the Native American party, a strongly nationalistic organization which had been briefly active during the 1840's. Now called the Know Nothing party, its basic principles were antiforeignism and anti-Roman Catholicism. The new party increased rapidly and had branches or wigwams throughout the United States. The year 1854 witnessed notable successes for the Know Nothings in many parts of the country. In Massachusetts they elected a governor, and they won control in Delaware also. In New York they polled 122,000 votes for governor, although they did not succeed in electing their candidate. The national congressional elections saw seventy-five Know Nothing congressmen seated.[23]

As the New Orleans city election of 1854 approached, the American press began to speak in favor of a new political force, the Independent Reform party. A notice appeared in the local press on March 14, 1854: "In order to secure Public Reform in our Municipal affairs, in an economical and thorough administration of our city government . . . the undersigned hereby call a City Convention to assemble on Lafayette Square on Thursday evening, March 16, 1854, at six o'clock,

[21]Overdyke, "History of the American Party in Louisiana," *loc. cit.*, XVI, 257.

[22]The last Whig candidate for president was General Winfield Scott, who ran in 1852. Locally and statewide, 1853 was the last year in which the Whig party made nominations.

[23]Follett, "The History of the Know Nothing Party in Louisiana," 24.

for the purpose of nominating irrespective of Party some of our best and most capable citizens to fill the various charter offices."[24] Of approximately six hundred signers less than fifteen had French names.[25]

Some Democrats immediately concluded that this was nothing more than the Whig party trying to resuscitate itself.[26] Many Creoles, however, identified it as the Know Nothings (Native Americans) in disguise. The Americans did not deny this but replied, "Bodysnatchers should not be afraid of ghosts," explaining that a party that raised whole graveyards to vote should not be afraid of rumors about the Know Nothings.[27] The *Propagateur Catholique* publicly announced that the movement was Know Nothing inspired and warned Catholics not to join. The publication did not "believe that any Creole would be willing to degrade himself by such an act of apostacy."[28]

At the same time that the Reformers ran their announcement of the mass meeting in Lafayette Square, there appeared in the *Daily True Delta* a lengthy exposé of the Know Nothing organization in New Orleans.

> The objects of the "Know Nothings," are twofold—part religious, part political; and the ends aimed at, the disfranchisement of adopted citizens, and their exclusion from office, and perpetual war upon the Catholic religion. With these for cardinal principles, the qualifications for membership and brotherhood are easily determined.
>
> *1st.* The applicant for admission to a "wigwam," must be a native born citizen, of native born parents, and not of the Catholic religion.
>
> *2nd.* To renounce all previously entertained political leanings, and co-operate exclusively with the new order.

[24] *Ibid.*, 21–22; *Commercial Bulletin*, March 14, 16, 1854.
[25] *Daily Orleanian*, March 15, 1854.
[26] *Louisiana Courier*, March 15, 1854.
[27] *Daily Crescent*, March 16, 1854. The Democrats had often been accused of voting the dead.
[28] *Louisiana Courier*, March 19, 1854, quoting the *Propagateur Catholique*.

*3rd.* To hold neither political, civil, nor religious intercourse with any person who is a Catholic; but, on the contrary, to use all available means to abolish political and religious privileges he may at present enjoy.

*4th.* That he will not vote for any man for office who is not a native citizen of the United States, or who may be disposed, if elected, to place any foreigner or Catholic in any office of emolument or trust—the latter not being, in the opinion of "Know Nothings," a credible witness, in any case, save where the oath is administered by his priest.

The "pass words" and "signs" for admission into the "wigwam" of the "Know Nothings," are as follows: The applicant raps at the outer door an indefinite number of times, asking at the close, in a low, whispering voice, "What meets here, today, (or night, as the case may be)?" The interrogated immediately replies, "I don't know," to which the applicant for admission responds, "I am one," and forthwith is admitted to a second door, at which he gives four distinct raps, when the door being opened, he whispers to its attendant, "Thirteen," and then advances into the body of the lodge.

If disposed to leave before the adjournment of the Lodge, the member leaving salutes the President, then the Vice President, by first placing his right hand on his heart, then letting it fall to his side, whispering to the guardian as he retires "thirteen."

If a member requires the assistance of a brother when mixing promiscuously with the public, he places the right forefinger upon the left eye-brow, as if in the act of scratching, looking directly at the person whose attention he desires to attract, when, if the person be a member, he is bound to respond immediately by a similar sign. If it be desired to know of a stranger whether he is of the initiated, on shaking hands with him the middle finger is placed upon the lowest joint of his little finger, next the wrist, with a gentle pressure; when, if he be a member, he will ask "Where did you get that?" to which he will rejoin, "I don't know;" and the querist will end by replying "I don't know either."

> Nothing concerning the association is to be committed to writing, or published; and the most profound silence and secrecy are to be observed by every "Know Nothing" outside; but every thing inside the Wigwam is imparted indiscriminately to members.
>
> Every member, on admission, swears by holding up his right hand, and pleages [*sic*] himself to do all in his power to put down foreign influence, and particularly the Catholic religion, and in no case to vote for any person for any office who is not a "native American citizen"; and no one, with some exceptions, is eligible to membership, unless he and both of his parents are native born.
>
> There are several Lodges, or Wigwams, at this time open—one, presided over by a Mr. H——ty, assembles in a room in the Mechanics' Institute, and another holds its meetings at No. 9, New Basin.[29] There are three degrees to be taken by members, between each, intervals of three weeks must occur.
>
> The New York Missionary who came here to organize the "Know Nothings" is styled "Judge Advocate," and he is charged with like duties in every other city in this section.
>
> As no records are kept, or publications made by the association, the plan of notifying members of any emergency requiring their speedy assembling is by scattering small square pieces of white paper over the banquettes and public thoroughfares, and by nailing them to posts, doors, or other places accessible to the public.[30]

The Americans defended their independent party on the ground that its purposes were to keep out those who would use parties for their own advantage and to cast off partisan shackles. They charged that the Democratic party perpetuated its power by corralling the immigrant vote and maintaining grog shops as polling places in order to keep decent people

[29]Both of these locations were uptown.
[30]*Daily True Delta,* March 15, 1854.

away. It was not right for a city the size of New Orleans to be governed by a comparative handful of foreigners who were ignorant of its laws and hardly spoke its language. The poor people should support law and order more than the rich, Americans maintained, for the rich could afford to buy protection, but the poor man could not. Instead of studying our institutions and waiting a while to take an active part, these Irish immigrants rushed headlong into politics as fast as they landed, aiding disorder and illegality. "The country must at last, . . . treat them as aliens," proclaimed the *Daily Crescent*, "if they will persist in not being Americans, nothing but Americans, and entitled to no more than all other Americans, even after being honestly naturalized."[31] The indignation of the "sons of the soil" was roused. The issue was drawn.

On March 22 the Democratic Creole *Louisiana Courier* openly stated that the American *Crescent* was one of the warmest friends of the Know Nothings and warned the foreign and Catholic elements of the city to beware. The *Crescent* insisted that there was no political nor religious question at stake, but a matter of justice and correction of misrule. But already in the American press there was practically open warfare against foreigners and Catholics.[32] At first the Americans pretended that the Independent movement was not a political party. They professed always to have considered parties in city government as "fooleries and abominations"[33] and could see no relation at all between national parties and municipal affairs. It was senseless to keep the same party in power on the local level because it was in power in Washington. What was the relation between men in Washington and the streets, levees, and gutters of New Orleans? Federal politics could not put out a fire or catch a thief or a housebreaker, or cleanse the town and prevent yellow fever. "Quit your party politics,

[31]*Daily Crescent*, March 21, 1854.
[32]*Ibid.*, March 23, 1854.
[33]*Ibid.*, March 16, 1854.

gentlemen! and go to work, not like factionists, but like men and citizens!"[34]

While vigorously denouncing parties, the Americans were urging utmost support of one. No longer able to use the Whig party as a means of opposition because of its national disintegration, they found the new nativist movement ideally suited to their purpose, for it struck at the very basis of the Creoles' local political power. When questioned about their former stand against independent movements, the Americans simply replied that they had changed their minds.[35] But the truth was that in 1852 the term "Independent" had meant Democrat (or Creole), while in 1854 the term "Independent" meant American.

In its inception the Know Nothing party was anti-Catholic as well as anti-immigrant in New Orleans. The Creoles labeled it "the anti-Catholic Native American movement."[36] The Catholics on the ticket were explained as a Know Nothing bid for the Whig vote below Canal Street. The party knew that it could not have the support of the lower sections' former Whigs without renominating officials such as Pilié and DeBuys, that no ticket could be formed without bearing the names of Creoles, by birth and by baptism Catholic. Though antiforeign, anti-Catholic, and anti-Creole in sentiment, the Know Nothing party by this method succeeded in drawing some members from those sections.[37]

The Germans, who for the most part were not Catholic, rejected the Know Nothing party solely on its anti-immigrant basis. They immediately recognized the Independent Reform ticket of 1854 as the Know Nothing party and saw "in the principles of the Democratic party the best surety for de-

[34] *Ibid.*, February 27, 1854. Cf. *Commercial Bulletin,* March 17, 22, 24, 1854.

[35] *Daily Crescent,* March 20, 1854.

[36] Follett, "The History of the Know Nothing Party in Louisiana," 19.

[37] *Louisiana Courier,* March 23, 27, 1854; Robert Clemens Reinders, "The Louisiana American Party and the Catholic Church," *Mid-America,* XL (New Series, XXIX [October, 1958]), 218 and *passim.*

feating the enemies of the people." They appealed, therefore, "urgently to all German citizens of New Orleans, to vote at the next municipal election the whole Democratic ticket, without any exception."[38]

The Creole-immigrant combination worked well again in the municipal election of 1854; the Democratic party drew its strength almost wholly from those sections of the city inhabited by these two groups. The Know Nothing vote was concentrated in the first, or American, district, while the fourth district, Lafayette, was divided between both parties, to the keen disappointment of the Americans. The "Irish channel" probably accounted for much of the Democratic vote in that section.

Democrat John L. Lewis, an old resident of the city who was closely associated with the Creoles, was elected mayor in 1854. His strength lay completely in the second, third, and fourth districts. In the first district the Independent Reform candidate, J. W. Breedlove, polled the sizable majority of five hundred votes; and all of the Independent's candidates for alderman won easily. The other districts elected all of the Democratic candidates except three assistant aldermen. The Democratic vote in the second (Creole) district was larger than it had been in 1852, demonstrating that many of the erstwhile Creole Whigs had switched to the Democratic party in an attempt to defeat the Americans.[39]

In all districts there were minorities, but the majority supported the party which represented its sectional interests. In the American sector immigrants in the "Irish channel" rejected the Know Nothing party and chose to stay with the Democrats. Similarly many of the former Creole Whigs, unable to bring themselves to join Democratic ranks, had no other choice than the American party. There were also people like Charles Gayarré, a Democrat, who went over to the Know Noth-

[38]*Louisiana Courier*, March 25, 1854; *Die Deutsche Zeitung*, March 25, 1854.

[39]*Daily Picayune*, March 29, 1854.

ing party in protest. He had personal grievances against the ruling clique of his party and did not approve of their fraudulent use of the immigrant vote.[40]

On election day, March 27, 1854, an incident occurred which set a pattern for much of the rest of the decade. Violence at one of the polls resulted in a stabbing. It had been rumored that the Democrats were going to march bands of voters from poll to poll and vote them over and over again in order to swell the Democratic numbers. The Independent Reform movement had been formed to stop this sort of thing; it was determined to do so. One of the polls to be attacked by these Democratic bands was the seventh precinct in the first ward of the first district, located at the O'Donnell ballroom at the corner of Circus (Rampart) and Poydras streets. Because of a rumor about much fraudulent voting there, the Independents decided to watch that poll carefully. According to the Know Nothings, twenty men who had already voted at the fourth precinct appeared at O'Donnell's and demanded to vote again. When they were refused, a fracas followed in which one man was stabbed in the back. The group was chased away, and it was said when the poll closed that the precinct's vote was 932, but the next morning it was announced as 1,400.[41] The party in power was accused of having done everything it could to get rid of the Independents who were challenging these illegal votes.[42]

A similar incident occurred about seven o'clock on election night. A band of men proceeded to a seventh ward poll after it had been called to their attention that no Reform men were witnessing the counting of the ballots. They re-

[40]Henry P. Dart (ed.), "Autobiography of Charles Gayarré," *Louisiana Historical Quarterly*, XII (January, 1929), 13; *Daily Crescent*, November 5, 1854. Gayarré had been passed over as the party's choice for nominee for congressman in 1853.

[41]Follett, "The History of the Know Nothing Party in Louisiana," 21–22.

[42]*Daily Crescent*, March 28, 1854; *Commercial Bulletin*, March 28, 1854; *Louisiana Courier*, March 28, 29, 30, 1854.

quested admittance but were refused, whereupon they battered open the door and were met by several pistol shots. No one was killed, but the chief of police, Stephen O'Leary, was wounded. At about four in the morning the rooms where the ballot boxes of the seventh ward had been deposited were broken into and their contents scattered in the street. The *Daily Crescent* reported several rows of a similar nature.[43]

In another instance in the seventh ward the Democrats, fearing they had lost the election there, seized control of many of the boxes and proceeded to count the ballots. The mob in front of the poll, where no Independent commissioner was allowed to participate in the counting, learned that 750 more votes had been cast than there were registered voters in the ward. The mob destroyed the ballot box.[44] Other cases were reported in which Irish Democrats forcibly took possession of the boxes. A city policeman was charged with breaking into one of the polling places and literally throwing out the Independent commissioners. It was said that enough fraudulent ballots were known at a few precincts to question majorities everywhere else. The common council had ceased legislating, the recorders had not heard any cases, and their police had left their thief-catching, "piously consigning our city to the care of God," while they took to electioneering.[45] The results of the election were not contested, however, except where the ballot boxes were destroyed. In these instances new elections were held, which resulted in Independent Reform victories.[46]

Both parties were accused of abducting sailors from ships or boarding houses and of forcing or paying them to vote. By this means a band of fifty or a hundred men could readily

[43]*Daily Crescent,* March 28, 1854; *Commercial Bulletin,* March 29, 1854.

[44]Overdyke, "History of the American Party in Louisiana," *loc. cit.,* XVI, 258. The *Louisiana Courier* of March 31, 1854, defended the Democratic tabulation in the seventh ward.

[45]*Daily Crescent,* March 28, 29, 1854.

[46]Follett, "The History of the Know Nothing Party in Louisiana," 22.

be procured to vote at any precinct in the city.[47] Apparently the Democrats got the Irish to do their dirty work, as it was always they who came in for the heaviest criticism. All of the commissioners and police in the districts where trouble occurred were said to be Irish, the illegal votes were supposedly cast by the Irish, and all of the lawbreaking was attributed to them. Yet election statistics indicate that the Creoles must have been their partners in crime, for the same candidates who carried the Irish immigrant districts also won in the Creole-populated precincts.[48]

Though the Americans had made inroads on the Democratic control of the municipal government, they by no means controlled the situation, even in their own district. It was after the 1854 municipal election that first district Recorder H. M. Summers resigned from the Democratic controlled police board because he was blocked in choosing policemen for his own district. The police force was an important part of the election machinery and without it no party's power could be complete.

By September of 1854 New Orleans had become the scene of bloody riots, assassinations, brawls, and street fights, chiefly between the immigrants and the Know Nothings. Armed gangs paraded through the streets after nightfall looking for encounters. Allegedly the trouble originated during the first week of September when a man killed a dog, and the owner demanded the watchman to arrest the man. When the watchman refused to do this, the indignation of the injured person's neighbors touched off the riot that was to last for many days in New Orleans. Participants were mostly professional hoodsmen and half-grown boys; watchmen prowled the streets at night armed with muskets and joined the gangs of ruffians.[49] The days were peaceful, but the hours of nightfall

[47]*Daily True Delta*, April 16, 1854; Follett, "The History of the Know Nothing Party in Louisiana," 58–59.

[48]*Daily Crescent*, March 30, 1854.

[49]Follett, "The History of the Know Nothing Party in Louisiana," 23.

were utterly disorderly. Men were attacked, beaten, and shot down; houses were gutted; and half-drunk armed bands paraded through the streets with threats and cries. It was said that the police not only failed to discourage these riots but actually participated in them.[50]

On one occasion Mayor Lewis, making a patrol of the city during the riot, at midnight encountered the former chief of police, Stephen O'Leary, armed with a musket and far from his home. The mayor finally persuaded him to give up his musket, although when O'Leary called the next day to collect it he spoke insultingly to Lewis.[51] Accounts were published of respectable men and women who were shot at on their own verandas by the ruffians. Wild rumors circulated that the Americans were out to burn the Catholic churches and to slaughter Catholics generally. Most of the initiative in these outbreaks seems to have been taken by the foreigners, especially the Irish. Even the Democratic mayor attempted to disperse crowds of Irishmen by telling them that Americans were not contemplating an attack.[52]

After a week of such rioting the mayor was finally obliged to recognize the inefficiency of the police force in dealing with the situation. He issued a proclamation calling for the enrollment of private citizens as a special civil police and placed a curfew of 8:00 P.M. on the entire city. About 250 citizens answered the call; divided into squads, they patrolled the city so effectively that a precarious peace was finally restored.[53] This newly formed police force arrested several of the ruffians, including O'Leary, who was charged with engaging in the riots, leading persons to commit acts of violence,

[50]*Daily Crescent*, September 12, 14, 1854; *Louisiana Courier*, September 15, 1854.

[51]*Daily Crescent*, September 16, 1854, quoting from the *Daily Delta.*

[52]Overdyke, "History of the American Party in Louisiana," *loc. cit.*, XVI, 259; *Daily Crescent*, September 18, 1854; *Commercial Bulletin*, September 16, 1854; *Louisiana Courier*, September 17, 1854.

[53]*Daily Crescent*, September 18, 1854; *Commercial Bulletin*, September 18, 1854; *Louisiana Courier*, September 20, 1854.

and constantly carrying concealed weapons. He posted bond and was released.[54]

The Americans severely criticized the Democratic administration, and even Mayor Lewis admitted that the police were divided and sectional. A single head was lacking, and there was much insubordination. The mayor thought the police department should be consolidated with one person at the head, with full responsibility.[55] These riots, while not the occasion of an election, marked the first bloody encounter between the Know Nothings and the Democrats. The sectional nature which the parties had assumed was revealed when the *Louisiana Courier* remarked that "it was unsafe for a citizen to appear in the streets above Canal street, unless he was recognized as a Whig or as one of the fraternity."[56]

Political activity for 1854 ended on November 17 with a seemingly unimportant election for a state senator and two state representatives. The following excerpt, however, shows that no longer would the Americans consider any election unimportant: "Little things grow out of great ones—oaks from acorns [*sic*]. If these primary elections are attended to, the great ones will go right; for in our government there is the same intimate connection between the different parts, that there is in a nice piece of machinery. The municipal elections are the smaller wheels, and the more easily moved. If they go right, all goes right; but if they are out of gear no amount of steam or patriotism can make a fitting compensation. Let the little wheels, therefore, be attended to. Let *every* man vote on every occasion."[57]

[54]*Daily Crescent,* September 19, 1854.

[55]*Ibid.,* October 5, 1854; *Commercial Bulletin,* September 14, October 3, 1854. This was how it was before 1853 when the mayor was head of the police department, but the Democrats in 1853 changed the control of the police from the mayor to a board in order to deprive the Whig mayor of his authority. Their plan now backfired on them.

[56]*Louisiana Courier,* September 26, 1854.

[57]*Daily Crescent,* November 27, 1854; *Semi-Weekly Creole,* November 25, 1854.

In this election the Democratic party was positively identified as anti-American. Of its candidates, the American *Creole*[58] said, "It is . . . their peculiar praise that they do not sympathize with Americans. This is significant of the position they occupy, and the agencies invoked to secure success."[59]

Apparently the "little wheels" were well oiled. In this election all of the Democratic candidates lost for the first time in two years. The reason for the Know Nothing victory was best expressed by the Democratic *Louisiana Courier*: "Their perfect organization, and thorough concert of action, gave them extraordinary facilities for bringing their adherents to the polls." The use of knives and pistols to control the polls was an equally contributing factor, according to the Creoles.[60]

Not only did the Democrats lose, they lost by heavy majorities. Their candidate for state senator received 1,565 votes, while the Know Nothing drew 3,830 votes. In the election for house members both candidates were from the American district. The contest in the first representative district resulted in 355 for the Know Nothing and 212 for the Democrat; in the fourth the Democrat received 146 to his opponent's 290.[61]

By 1852 the American section of New Orleans was willing to reunify the city provided its interests were sufficiently protected. From the Americans' point of view, the other two sections had brought New Orleans to the verge of bankruptcy. Incorporating the town of Lafayette gave the Americans room for growth. In the years immediately after consolidation the immigrant vote there was sometimes larger than the American, and the Creoles won the foreigners over to their Democratic coalition. The Americans, finding themselves without an organization after the Whig party's dissolution, faced political oblivion. Events called for immediate and decisive action. The

[58]The *Creole* was a small sheet which was rabidly pro-American.
[59]*Louisiana Courier*, November 26, 1854, quoting from the *Creole*.
[60]*Louisiana Courier*, November 29, 1854.
[61]*Daily Crescent*, November 28, 1854.

revival of the Native American party, with its anti-immigrant plank, furnished them a ready weapon with which to fight their way to political domination.

CHAPTER FOUR

# *The Triumph of Sam*

HEARTENED by their successful rout of the Democrats in the state election of 1854, the New Orleans wigwam of the American party, as the Native American or Know Nothing party was called, continued to expand until by the end of 1855 it was the most powerful political force in the city. Little is known of the inner workings of the party during this time, for it was still a secret organization, keeping no records and publishing nothing. Nevertheless, its objective was clear—to reduce the swollen Democratic majorities of the second (Creole) and third (immigrant) districts.

The first political activity of 1855 occurred in early spring with the election of members to the city's common council. Although this was an off-year election, the Americans realized the importance of placing their candidates. In spite of the inroads made on the Democratic majority in the municipal election of 1854, the government remained essentially in the hands of the Democrats. If the council could be filled with Know Nothings, control of the legislative branch of the municipal government would be theirs. Then they could appoint the election commissioners, who determined the electorate in New Orleans in the 1850's.

The Americans emphasized that choosing city council members was of more importance to New Orleans than electing legislators or United States congressmen, for council members' influence on the city's welfare was great. Proper management of municipal business could increase the wealth, prosperity, and volume of trade in New Orleans. With so much at stake, it was important that the council consist of able, intelligent, and reliable men. Members should be residents and property-holders, not too conservative to advance, but not so progressive as to run wild and pursue visionary schemes. The American party urgently appealed to businessmen to step out into the ranks and supervise the election.[1] The time had come for the city to have men who were identified with its prosperity and who represented all. In previous councils many important interests, especially those of commercial uptown New Orleans, were completely without representation.[2]

From the American point of view it was an absolute necessity to gain control of the city government in order to rescue it from a deplorable financial condition. With no money in the treasury, cash warrants were selling daily at a discount. The employees of the city were frequently unable to obtain their scanty wages when they were due and had to petition the city on numerous occasions for payment. The first council (Whig) after consolidation had redeemed the city's credit. Soon municipal bonds were selling at a premium, all debts were paid, and a surplus of cash existed in the treasury.[3]

In the spring of 1853 the Democrats obtained absolute majorities in both branches of the council. When they came into power there were $500,000 in the treasury and no outstanding obligations; within a year they spent the surplus and incurred $500,000 of indebtedness, which they left to their successors. They were also responsible for a consistent rise in taxes. These criticisms were strongly reminiscent of the charges made by the American district against the Creole and immigrant municipalities during the consolidation struggle. The Independent Reform movement of 1854 won control of the assistant board of aldermen, but the Democrats still held the board of aldermen and the entire executive branch. American commercial interests expected no reform and therefore worked for a complete change of administration.[4]

[1]*Daily Crescent,* March 10, 1855; *Commercial Bulletin,* March 26, 1855.
[2]*Daily Crescent,* March 14, 1855; *Commercial Bulletin,* March 16, 19, 1855.
[3]*Daily Crescent,* March 22, 1855. [4]*Ibid.*

Precaution and preparedness became the bywords of the Know Nothing party from its inception in New Orleans. About a week before the March, 1855, election, the party chiefs warned:

> A deep and well matured scheme has been silently and secretly concocted. The only hope of a triumph is based upon the expectation that confidence on the part of our friends may beget carelessness and apathy, and that on the day of election we may be unprepared for a united and powerful rally of the opposition. When, therefore, we bid the supporters and upholders of good government be on their guard; when we warn them of the necessity of thorough organization, and unceasing vigilance; when we tell them that they must leave no point unprotected, no avenue unwatched; . . . that above all, they must be fully prepared to baffle all attempts at fraud, and destroy the machinations of evil-minded and designing party leaders—we are far from repeating the hackneyed slogans of political strife, but are uttering our serious, well-considered and sincere convictions.[5]

Each party printed its own official ballots and in addition often distributed at the polls false, unofficial tickets for the opposition, which were invalid and would not be counted. On the eve of the election voters were urged to examine their tickets very carefully before putting them in the ballot boxes for, as the editor of the *Daily Crescent* warned, fraudulent and deceptive tickets would be "as thick as leaves in autumn."[6]

Until the very day of election the Independent Reformers emphasized that they had not accomplished their goal. Only one half of one of the two branches of the city government was theirs. Reform must be completed. Know Nothings were to be at the polls early and remain there until the results were "fairly and honestly proclaimed."[7] The Democrats scoffed at the Independents' use of the word reform.[8]

[5]*Bee*, March 20, 1855; *Daily Crescent*, March 21, 1855.
[6]*Daily Crescent*, March 26, 1855.
[7]*Ibid.*, March 25, 26, 1855.
[8]*Louisiana Courier*, March 24, 25, 1855.

The election was a complete victory for the American party, which voted thirty-four out of thirty-five candidates into office. The day was quiet. Know Nothings constantly guarded the polls and excluded foreigners with questionable naturalization papers. From opening to closing bands of spectators scrutinized the voting and did not think of home or rest until all the ballots were counted and all fraud or trickery placed beyond possibility. It was reported that there was no drinking, gasconading, crowding, jostling, or hustling around the polls. The Americans felt that it was an election of which the city could be proud and hoped to see it imitated. They attributed victory to the presence of "Sam," the "somewhat famous personage [who] was distinctly visible in various parts of the city. . . . As will be seen by reference to the election returns, he created quite a sensation during the day."[9] The Democrats accused the Americans of illegally refusing to admit naturalized citizens to the polls.[10]

The Americans emerged from the contest of March, 1855, in control of the legislative branch of the city government, and the situation of 1853 was reversed. At that time the executive department was Whig, and the legislative Democratic. Now the city's chief executive was a Democrat, and the lawmakers were Know Nothings. In less than a month after the election the Americans impeached the two Democratic recorders, P. Seuzeneau and C. Ramos, for malfeasance in office. The charge was that they illegally allowed their subordinates to receive fees for Negro passes and bonds. The city charter provided that no officer under impeachment could exercise his office until the issue was settled. The Americans took advantage of the opportunity by replacing the Democrats with two members of their own party. This made the police board Know Nothing by a count of four to one, since the mayor was the only Democrat. The Creoles immediately charged that the whole affair was a ruse to make possible the creation

[9] *Daily Crescent*, March 27, 1855.
[10] *Ibid.*; *Commercial Bulletin*, March 27, 1855; *Louisiana Courier*, March 28, 1855.

of a Know Nothing police force. At the first meeting under the new arrangement it was obvious to Mayor Lewis that he was the fifth wheel on the wagon, and he left. The recorders promptly appointed a completely American police force, which they reorganized for greater efficiency.[11]

The summer of 1855 found the Know Nothing party a well-established part of the political machinery of New Orleans. Although the organization, proceedings, and membership of the party were at this time still secret, it appears from later information that the nucleus of the party's strength was the neighborhood ward club. Good discipline at this level insured large turnouts and control of the polls.[12]

By late spring the city Whig organ, the *Daily Crescent*, was willing to admit that its party was dead. On May 11, 1855, it said, "The late Whig party gives forth no tokens of life–no evidences of vitality–no signs of resurrection." Henceforth the American press concentrated its efforts on advancing the fortune of the new political organization.

The Know Nothing party was an attempt to divert the increasing agitation over the slavery issue by fanning the flames of religious and national prejudice. Adherence to the Constitution and absolute silence summed up the party's stand on slavery. This plank furnished no difficulty for the party in Louisiana or New Orleans, as southerners in general felt quite safe with it. Some parts of the platform, however, were quite distasteful to New Orleanians. One was the secrecy that surrounded the party in its inception. This did not last long, for by early July, 1855, public mass meetings were announced in the American press. Local members rejoiced when this happened.[13]

The religious plank caused the most trouble in New Orleans. Members were required to pledge themselves to do everything in their power to keep Catholics out of political of-

[11]*Daily Crescent*, April 9, 13, 26, 1855; *Commercial Bulletin*, April 9, 10, 1855; *Louisiana Courier*, April 8, 1855.

[12]*Daily Crescent*, May 1–30, 1858.

[13]*Ibid.*, July 9, 1855. This was the result of a decision at the national level for open meetings.

fice. Local Know Nothings settled this issue early. In June, 1855, a man named Broom came from the North to reorganize the party; in so doing he threw out Catholic and Jewish Creoles. Known as the Blue Book, or Simon Pure segment, Broom's group contained only a minority of the party's members and never controlled New Orleans. In the subsequent state convention held in New Orleans on July 4, 1855, the Know Nothing party of Louisiana repudiated the religious plank and reorganized itself. From then on the Blue Book or Simon Pure wing had virtually no power in the state.[14]

The rejection of the religious plank by Louisiana brought up the whole question of the relationship between the state and parent organization. Louisiana tested its right to change national policy when it sent Charles Gayarré, a Creole Catholic, to the New York convention as a delegate from New Orleans. Gayarré addressed the convention as follows: "We are imperatively and unequivocally instructed, gentlemen, not to affiliate with you, if you retain in your constitution and in your oath *the slightest allusion to any religion whatever.* In relation to the Catholics of Louisiana, I have endeavored to demonstrate to you that they are free from those gross superstitions which you attribute to the church of Rome. . . . We acknowledge no other power in the head of our church than one which is purely spiritual. . . . Louisianians are enlightened Catholics, who would not permit the most distant ecclesiastical interference with politics."[15]

The convention refused admission to Gayarré, and the Louisiana delegation withdrew. Upon returning home, Gayarré addressed what he called an "immense meeting" in the ballroom of the Orleans Theatre. He urged prompt dissolution of the party "on whose banners . . . was read an inscription in letters as awful as those which flamed luridly on the walls of the Babylonian palace—'Political disabilities, religious test, no liberty of conscience, no equality of rights among native

[14]Follett, "The History of the Know Nothing Party in Louisiana," 35–36; *Commercial Bulletin,* July 6, 7, 1855; *Louisiana Courier,* July 7, 1855.

[15]*Daily True Delta,* September 18, 1855.

born Americans.' "[16] In September of 1855, just nine months after he joined, Gayarré left the party. He gave as his reason that the original intention of the Know Nothings had been to put down incapacity, greed, and corruption in government. This purpose had disappeared, however, and "since there was 'but a like repetition of like practices' and 'a deplorable renovation' of the 'demoralization and system of rewards for political subserviency he felt that he should withdraw from the party.' "[17] Soon the party declined in the state. In New Orleans, on the other hand, it thrived, for it symbolized the Americans' determination to overcome the Creole-immigrant coalition.

Even though New Orleans Know Nothings officially repudiated the religious plank of the platform, their party continued for some time to have an anti-Catholic reputation. The Roman church admonished its members under most severe penalties to have nothing to do with it. Threats like the following from the church hierarchy even appeared in the public press:

> We do not believe there is a Catholic–meaning thereby, one who has not made himself liable to the penalty of excommunication for not fulfilling his Easter duties–who has been or is a member of the Dark Lantern faction in Louisiana. We do not believe there is a member of the order who, if he were to die without repentance and retraction, would be entitled to Christian burial, according to the solemn rites of the Church. This endeavor, by virtual apostates, to get Catholic support by calling themselves Catholics, when they know they are not properly entitled to the name, illustrates most forcibly the duplicity and low cunning that has characterized the order in all its sneaking and contemptible policy. If any nominal Catholic, who has not had the grace to live according to the commands of his Church, and

[16]Dart (ed.), "Autobiography of Charles Gayarré," *loc. cit.*, XII, 16.

[17]Overdyke, "History of the American Party in Louisiana," *loc. cit.*, XVI, 269, quoting the Opelousas *Courier*, October 6, 1855. See also Charles Gayarré, *Address to the People of Louisiana on the State of Parties* (New Orleans, 1855), 37.

> has therefore, been deprived of the inestimable blessing of her Sacraments, has been beguiled into joining the order, he may deny it with his lips, but cannot in his heart, that by so doing he has entered the ranks of the sworn enemies of the Church, and must be regarded, by every practical Catholic, as among her most dangerous foes. There are many young men who believe fully in the doctrines of the Church—who would shudder with horror at the thought of a deathbed bereft of her Holy Sacraments, and who would willingly *die* for her, although they have not had the grace to *live* for her. You will find none of these among the Know-Nothings. Their vote, whether they be Whigs or Democrats, will be given without an exception, to the Democratic ticket, for, we repeat, that *in this election*, at least, the Democratic ticket is the only one not pledged to religious proscription and hostility to the Catholic Church.[18]

Most of the Creole press also joined in warning the Catholics that the Know Nothing party was inimical to their religion.[19]

Americans denied the anti-Catholic allegations and used their rejection of the religious plank as proof of their sincerity. They emphasized their resolution of July 12, 1855, which said "that we are the friends of religion as well as civil liberty, and that we are opposed to any political proscription for religious faith, either as to the right of voting or holding office."[20] They presented such prominent Catholic Creoles as William DeBuys, who expressed his full approval of and intention to vote the Know Nothing ticket. The *Daily Crescent* recommended his letter to the "earnest consideration of all searchers after truth—especially to our friends down

[18]*Semi-Weekly Creole,* October 31, 1855, quoting the *Southern Standard,* October 28, 1855. The *Southern Standard* was a New Orleans Catholic newspaper. The *Semi-Weekly Creole,* a Know Nothing sheet, was emphatically opposed to Catholic interference in politics and used such quotations as the above to prove actual church intervention. Follett, "The History of the Know Nothing Party in Louisiana," 43.

[19]*Louisiana Courier,* October 15, 21, 1855.

[20]Overdyke, "History of the American Party in Louisiana," *loc. cit.,* XVI, 269.

town."[21] They pointed also to the Know Nothing candidate for governor of Louisiana, Charles Derbigny,[22] who was a Catholic and yet was their most prominent nominee.[23] These were renegade Catholics, the Creoles answered. They could not possibly be good Catholics and adhere to the Know Nothing or American party. Evidence for this position was an oath signed reputedly by John Huffty, Know Nothing candidate for sheriff, that he would never vote for a Catholic for office. The Creoles tried to chide him into public avowal or denial. When he refused to do either, his opponents were sure that he had signed it and that the party was anti-Catholic.[24]

The truth of the matter was that in New Orleans the Know Nothing party was anti-Catholic, for its main strength lay above Canal Street, the stronghold of Protestantism.[25] This section was fighting downtown New Orleans, which comprised Creoles and immigrants, who were predominantly Catholic. As a political organization it tried to attract all voters. Since there were many votes to be had in the second and third districts, the party repudiated open religious proscription. Nevertheless, religion played an important role in the battle.

In discussions of religion and the Know Nothing party in New Orleans the position of Adrian Rouquette, a Catholic priest, is often cited to show a sympathetic feeling between the Catholic church and the party. Rouquette, using the pseudonym Mucius, published a pamphlet entitled *La Question Americaine* (New Orleans, 1855) in which he said that perhaps a Know Nothing victory in Louisiana would not be too bad if it killed the anti-Catholic plank by illustrating to the parent organization that the party could succeed without

[21]*Daily Crescent*, October 30, 1855.
[22]Derbigny ran for governor in November, 1855.
[23]Follett, "The History of the Know Nothing Party in Louisiana," 38.
[24]*Louisiana Courier*, October 25, 1855.
[25]Robert Clemens Reinders, "Orestes A. Brownson's Visit to New Orleans, 1855," *Louisiana Historical Quarterly*, XXXVIII (July, 1955), 4 and *passim.*

religious proscription. Rouquette was not advocating Know Nothingism; he was saying that, if a Louisiana victory could relieve the condemnation of the church nationally, it would serve a good purpose. His concern was for the church and not for the principles or success of the American party.[26]

Political activity in New Orleans revived with the fall election of state and parish officers. Doubtless the action of the Louisiana delegation in the New York convention of June, 1855, helped local Know Nothings. Aware of this fact, the Democratic central committee asked the American central committee shortly before the election to co-operate with it in appointing inspectors[27] who would agree to respect the opinion of several "eminent jurists." The Americans wanted none of this, for they knew the "eminent jurists" were Democrats, except for one. They, therefore, rejected the offer.[28] The Democrats needed such a compromise, for the council was Know Nothing and would appoint most of the election commissioners.

Constantly the Know Nothings called the attention of the election commissioners to cases of fraudulent naturalization. Such certificates were to be rejected. In one case the courts issued naturalization papers during the summer recess.[29] These were considered null and void, and men who obtained such certificates were not to be allowed to vote. In another case numerous citizenship papers had been issued by the clerk of the second district court but were not recorded in the court journals. These, too, were invalid.[30] The fears of the Americans in respect to fraudulent naturalizations were well-founded, for in the first three months of 1855 alone 7,173 im-

[26]Overdyke, "History of the American Party in Louisiana," *loc. cit.*, XVI, 271.

[27]The party which controlled the selection of inspectors or commissioners was generally victorious. The commissioners decided who could vote, and since the political balance hinged on the choice of which immigrants could, the commissioner assumed a key position.

[28]*Daily Crescent*, October 17, 1855; *Commercial Bulletin*, October 17, 1855; *Louisiana Courier*, October 17, 18, 19, 1855.

[29]Follett, "The History of the Know Nothing Party in Louisiana," 44.

[30]*Daily Crescent*, November 3, 1855; *Commercial Bulletin*, November 2, 1855.

migrants arrived in New Orleans, many of whom remained. It was not uncommon for a local court to naturalize as many as two hundred people a day, most of whom fulfilled none of the requirements. On November 1, 1855 (All Saints Day, a great Catholic holiday), the courts remained open all day in order that the number of voters might be increased.[31] Almost without exception these immigrant votes were cast for the Democratic party. Their opponents grew increasingly determined to stop such frauds.

The Americans were confident as the election approached, for they now felt they could handle rowdyism at the polls. To those voters who might stay away from the polls from fear of disorder came a pledge that they "need not be in the slightest degree apprehensive of disturbances. These things will be prevented. Americans will be on guard, and as they never commence riotings, they will be prompt to put down rioters. This assurance ought to be sufficient to satisfy all sensible men."[32]

Balloting on Monday, November 5, resulted in another sweeping victory for the Know Nothings. In all districts except the fourth (Lafayette) the American candidate for governor received a majority vote, as did their candidates for the state senate. In the contest for state representatives the Americans placed almost all of their candidates, and they were completely victorious in the election for sheriff and other parish officers. In each case victory meant drastically reducing the number of votes in the second (Creole) and third (immigrant) districts.[33] This was accomplished either by invalidating questionable naturalization papers or by outright intimidation of Democratic voters at the polls. Democratic victories in Lafayette indicate that the Americans allowed the election there to proceed unhindered, perhaps because of the small total vote in that district.

[31]Overdyke, "History of the American Party in Louisiana," *loc. cit.*, XVI, 273.

[32]*Daily Crescent*, November 3, 1855; *Commercial Bulletin*, November 2, 1855.

[33]*Daily Picayune*, November 7, 1855.

For United States congressmen the city also gave a majority to the Know Nothing candidates. The first district, New Orleans below Canal Street plus Plaquemines and St. Bernard parishes, was no problem. With the size of the Democratic vote in the second and third municipal districts reduced by force and violence, the rest came easily. St. Bernard returned a total of thirty votes and all but two or three were for the Know Nothing candidate. Plaquemines was more evenly divided, but the Know Nothings won there also. In fact, after the Know Nothing party conquered the second and third municipal districts, the first congressional district was practically a pocket borough of the Americans. It was the second congressional district, New Orleans above Canal Street and LaFourche Parish, that presented difficulties. The city uptown was American and the Know Nothings had a large majority there; but the sugar parish of LaFourche, essentially Catholic, refused to vote for the renegade Catholic Derbigny and his ticket. Neither did it return T. G. Hunt, the American incumbent, to Congress.[34] The first (American) municipal district was not large enough to offset the rural vote, and thus the stronghold of Know Nothingism in New Orleans was represented by a Democrat in the United States House of Representatives.

The American ticket as a whole lost the state by a margin of some three thousand votes. The Know Nothing Creole Catholic, Charles Derbigny, received little support from the traditionally Democratic Protestant northern parishes. The southern Catholic parishes would not vote for him because he was an apostate Catholic.[35]

In New Orleans the election was probably the most riotous ever, with the Know Nothings having things much their own way. Immigrants had a hard time getting to the polls. Often the only approach was a narrow alley; jostling and fights occurred before they even got there. At one poll a spy,

[34]*Ibid.*

[35]Overdyke, "History of the American Party in Louisiana," *loc. cit.*, XVI, 276-77.

stationed on a scantling above, looked down to see which way the immigrants voted. If they did not vote the right ticket, the watcher cried, "Initiate him." As the man emerged, he was beaten. Whenever they could, the Know Nothing election commissioners refused to recognize naturalization papers which they believed were illegally granted. The Democrats resorted to "protest boxes" for votes that were refused, having printed slips for that purpose before the election. The Know Nothing commissioners refused to recognize the validity of these slips, as the law made no provision for them. Fraud was rampant on both sides. On the defensive, the Democrats used every means possible to gain the vote. But the Americans were determined to keep the Democratic vote down; often the cry was heard, "Clear the polls, you damned Dutch and Irish Sons of Bitches!"[36]

Above Canal Street the election was, on the whole, peaceful. Below Canal it was turbulent, particularly in the third district. In the seventh and ninth wards, traditional Democratic strongholds, ballot boxes were broken, opened, or carried off. Bands of armed men, some in carriages, some on horseback, passed through the streets hurrahing for "Sam." They killed at least one Irishman, John Reilly, who was standing at the corner of Victory and Ingheim streets. Someone made remarks and the occupants of the carriages opened fire, discharging about eighteen or twenty shots. It was reported that a crowd known as the Mobile contingent came to New Orleans in a mail boat to aid their fellow Know Nothings. Supposedly Memphis and other river towns also furnished gangs of ruffians to assist in the election.[37]

The Creoles were bitter. They printed American press releases which said, "The time has passed when there can be bullying at the polls." To this the Creoles asked, "Do you intend to be understood as speaking seriously, or is the above sentence a mere sarcasm?" To them the election was nothing

[36]*Ibid.*, 275–76; *Louisiana Courier*, November 6, 1855.

[37]Follett, "The History of the Know Nothing Party in Louisiana," 46; *Commercial Bulletin*, November 8, 1855.

but one bullying affair after another at almost every precinct.[38] They said that the American police force "either joined the Skinners . . . or looked on unmoved while the bowie-knife of the murderers replaced the laws of the State."[39] The Americans were satisfied with the verdict of the people and would stand on that. They insisted that disturbances in the various districts were in direct proportion to the number of foreign-born policemen. Allegedly, when native American policemen were in a majority, hardly any disturbances occurred.[40]

Because of the riotous election and the destruction of many ballot boxes, the Democrats contested many of the results. John Huffty, sheriff-elect who defeated the Democratic candidate John Bell, was one of the most prominent of those challenged. At least nine hundred votes were presumed destroyed in the seventh and ninth precincts, both Democratic strongholds. If these had been added to Bell's number, he would have been elected. Hence his party brought the case to the first district court, which by state law had jurisdiction. The judge of that court, however, had American leanings, and the Democrats preferred to bring the complaint before a more sympathetic tribunal. Therefore, instead of basing their case on a contested election, they sued for a writ of mandamus to compel the commissioners to estimate returns for the missing boxes. Democratic Judge John B. Cotton issued the writ in a courtroom filled with armed adherents of both sides. When the American commissioners refused to comply, they were fined and imprisoned.[41]

The Democrats were now forced to bring the case to the first district court as a contested election. Both sides claimed fraud, but the decision was rendered in favor of Huffty, and the governor issued his commission. The matter was not al-

[38]*Louisiana Courier*, November 9, 1855.

[39]*Daily Delta*, November 13, 1855.

[40]*Daily Crescent*, November 9, 17, 20, 1855; *Commercial Bulletin*, November 6, 1855.

[41]Kendall, *History of New Orleans*, I, 211; Overdyke, "History of the American Party in Louisiana," *loc. cit.*, XVI, 409–10.

lowed to rest, however, for at the next meeting of the Democratic-controlled state legislature Huffty was removed from office by that body, and the commission was given to Bell. When Huffty refused to surrender the office, Bell opened an office on St. Ann Street, in the Pontalba building. For two weeks New Orleans enjoyed the protection of two sheriffs. The supreme court finally upheld the action of the state legislature in favor of Bell, and Huffty was forced to capitulate.[42]

The contest for the sheriff's office was only one of many which filled the court dockets after the 1855 election. Almost all of the returns by which a Democratic candidate was defeated were contested. In each case the lower court decided in favor of the American candidate, only to be reversed by the Democratic supreme court. This led the Americans to advocate new elections in the case of contested returns, while the Democrats sought court decisions.[43] In view of the constant reversals by the supreme court, the Americans concluded that victory in 1856 depended upon their absolute control of the polls without the destruction of ballot boxes.

The capture of the municipal government by the Know Nothings in 1855 amounted almost to revolution. Violence was common throughout the city. In 1856 the Americans consolidated their gains, and their party became more latitudinarian. It abandoned the policy of secrecy and adopted a more conciliatory tone toward Catholic and naturalized citizens.[44]

On several occasions Americans publicized their change of attitude. In January, 1856, the Creoles charged Americans with discriminating against Catholics in the appointment of public school faculties. Rumor had it that a number of teachers had been dismissed because they were Catholic. One of the American members of the school board wrote an article in which

[42]Overdyke, "History of the American Party in Louisiana," *loc. cit.*, XVI, 409–10; *Daily Crescent*, March 16, April 8, 1856.

[43]*Louisiana Courier*, November 7, 1855; *Daily Crescent*, November 8, 1855; Overdyke, "History of the American Party in Louisiana," *loc. cit.*, XVI, 410–11.

[44]Follett, "The History of the Know Nothing Party in Louisiana," 61.

he denied that religion had entered into the appointments or dismissals. He admitted that six teachers had not been rehired but insisted that three of them were Protestant. He explicitly charged the Democrats with trying to influence the spring election by making the Americans appear to be anti-Catholic.[45] Another opportunity for the Americans to dissociate religion and politics came early in 1856 when the Know Nothing *Daily Crescent* reviewed a book entitled *Americanism versus Romanism*, by James L. Chapman. Condemning the book bitterly, the reviewer charged that it was written for the purpose of exciting religious and political feeling. It carried the doctrines of Americanism from the political scene to the religious, where they had no business. Surely readers would have little interest or sympathy with such a work.[46]

Efforts of the New Orleans wigwam to include Catholics in the party was not confined to local action. At the national convention of 1856 in Philadelphia George Eustis of New Orleans made a two-hour speech in which he said that Louisiana could not accept Article VIII, the anti-Catholic plank. He assured the convention that any Louisiana member who professed Roman Catholicism was required to deny allegiance to any temporal power not cognizable in the state and in the United States. The party required a solemn pledge of each member that he would never divulge any secrets; each Catholic in Louisiana had taken that pledge. On the strength of this the Louisiana delegation was seated.[47]

The state party replaced the eighth plank of the platform with this question: "Would you consider yourself by your religion, or under any circumstances, bound to reveal the secrets of this association?" This applied to any situation including deathbed confessionals. Louisiana Know Nothings were required to take this oath: "I will never betray the secrets of this society to any one but a member of the American Order, and

[45] *Daily Crescent*, January 7, 1856.
[46] *Ibid.*, May 26, 1856.
[47] Overdyke, "History of the American Party in Louisiana," *loc. cit.*, XVI, 419.

I will vote for none but native-born Americans for office. . . . I will not favor any religious distinction; but will oppose the interference of the priest of any religious denomination with political affairs of the country."[48] The national party retained the original anti-Catholic plank.

Besides attempting to make peace with the Roman Catholic element of New Orleans, the Know Nothings effected a reconciliation with the foreigners. In their state convention of June, 1856, they passed a resolution "that in foreign affiliation we reject none, whether native or foreign whose judgment and sympathies are with us upon the principles we seek to inforce, believing that all interests will be promoted in the end by our success."[49]

By spring of 1856 the Know Nothing party had either incorporated or crushed its opposition. A month before the municipal elections of that year the American press recorded political "lethargy and supineness" among its rivals. Feigning bewilderment over such a situation, the Americans looked for signs of activity, for they knew the contest would be warm and determined—the most exciting in the city's history.[50] Their press betrayed its pretended perplexity when it observed that even though little had been heard from the Democrats, surely that party would put up candidates. How could a contest be "warm and spirited" when there might not even be an opposing ticket?

On May 16, about three weeks before the election, the Americans announced their ticket. The candidate for mayor was Charles M. Waterman, who was hailed as the first merchant nominee ever put forward. He was typical of the well-to-do Americans who seem to have controlled the party in its early years in New Orleans.[51] For comptroller they nomi-

[48]Follett, "The History of the Know Nothing Party in Louisiana," 69–70.

[49]Overdyke, "History of the American Party in Louisiana," *loc. cit.*, XVI, 419.

[50]*Daily Crescent,* May 7, 1856; *Commercial Bulletin,* May 31, 1856.

[51]Little or nothing is known of the men who held the reins of the party locally in the first three years of its existence.

nated Thomas Theard and for street commissioner, P. Amadée Guyol. Candidates for recorder were: first district, Gerard Stith; second, J. L. Favre; third, Joseph Solomon; and fourth, François Bouligny. Creole names were well represented in the American slate of candidates, thus giving further evidence of the new policy of the party.[52]

The Democrats were in serious trouble. An internal feud had developed which almost split the party openly. For a while its members could not even agree on whether the party should present candidates.[53] Finally, on May 15, the Democrats were able to announce their slate: mayor, Willian A. Elmore; comptroller, J. R. Macmurdo; street commissioner, J. A. D'Hemencourt; and recorders for the four districts—Peter B. Taylor, first; Clement Ramos, second; P. Seuzeneau, third; and Henry Jackson, fourth.[54]

The campaign followed the usual pattern. The Democrats said that the streets and public grounds of the city were in a state of ruinous decay, that the jail houses, courthouses, and engine houses were in a terrible condition, and that every plank road in the city was rotten. Every avenue to the wharves was impassable when it rained, and the workhouse was a shame to the city. The Americans refuted the charges. They had never known the public grounds of the city to be as beautiful as now. Complaints about the streets were perennial. Public buildings, however, were in good repair, and most important of all, the council had paid the floating debt and established the credit of the city. To have done any more would have been an extravagance.

An attempt to revive the old political trick of vote-swapping enlivened the campaign. The Democrats offered to vote for the American candidates for mayor and comptroller, if their opponents would support the Democratic aldermanic candidates. The Americans would have none of this; they expected to capture both the executive and legislative branches. For a

[52]*Daily Crescent,* May 16, 1856.
[53]Follett, "The History of the Know Nothing Party in Louisiana," 80.
[54]*Louisiana Courier,* May 15, 1856; *Daily Delta,* May 20, 1856.

party to elect only the mayor was an empty victory, since experience proved that the group dominating the council controlled the government. If this was an attempt at compromise by the Creoles, it was unlikely that such one-sided terms would be accepted.

As usual, the Know Nothings harped on fradulent naturalizations, a whole series of which, they claimed, were performed by unauthorized district courts.[55] They expected the hospitals, lockups, parish prison, and workhouse to be emptied to swell the Democratic ranks. "Wash them, shave them, and dress them up with a little decency," sneered the *Daily Crescent*, "and four or five hundred votes may be thus manufactured!" The Democrats, sure that the Americans would use their former tactics, repeatedly reminded their supporters that they must guard against unlawful disfranchisement.[56]

The election resulted in a complete Know Nothing victory. Every candidate of the party won. For the first time the Americans dominated both the executive and legislative branches of the city government. They controlled the police and the election commissioners, and thereby the polls. By the same means employed in the 1855 election, they succeeded in reducing the Democratic vote in the second and third districts by two-thirds.[57]

Bloodshed, violence, and death were the order of the day. A general melee was reported in the third and seventh precincts. In the eleventh two Sicilians not authorized to vote were refused by the commissioner. When they called for help, a riot ensued in which many were wounded and two were killed. Norbert Trepagnier, clerk of the first district court, was stabbed almost to death. The poll was closed at once, and a general search for the band of Sicilians was instituted; the two leaders were found and killed immediately. Most of this violence occurred in the second district; the third was the

[55]*Daily Crescent,* May 27, 28, 29, 1856.
[56]*Ibid.,* May 7, 31, June 2, 1856; *Louisiana Courier,* May 28, June 1, 2, 1856.
[57]*Daily Picayune,* June 5, 1856.

most peaceful during the election. There were several disturbances in the fourth, but none were serious.[58]

The Democrats immediately charged fraud and intimidation. They said that armed men occupied some of the polls and dictated who could vote. The Americans did not attempt to deny participation in the turmoil. Instead they reminded the Democrats that it was they who had initiated the corruption of the ballot box by illegal use of the foreign vote. They must now take the consequences.[59] Americans recalled that Democratic leaders never complained of crime when it advanced the success of their party.[60]

The Americans explained the drastic reduction of the Democratic vote on the grounds that the election date had been changed from April to June, at which time at least one thousand voters were absent from the city. That it was mostly Americans who left the city was blithely ignored. The Know Nothings further claimed that their opponents refused to support the machine candidate of their party, disregarding the years during which the Democrats had backed a city political machine. Intraparty strife undoubtedly decreased their strength at the polls.

The Know Nothing explanation of the lack of Democratic votes in the third, or foreign, district was probably the most rational offered. They said that at least a thousand naturalized citizens stayed away from the polls because they had at last realized that alliance with the Creoles had done them little good.[61] The editor of the *Daily Orleanian*, Democratic organ of the third district, had been afraid of this, for in a pre-election editorial he expressed apprehension over the lack of interest the foreigners were taking in the forthcoming election. The immigrants considered it a struggle between the natives, of

[58] *Daily Crescent*, June 3, 1856; *Commercial Bulletin*, June 3, 11, 1856; *Louisiana Courier*, June 4, 1856.

[59] *Daily Crescent*, June 11, 1856; *Louisiana Courier*, June 10, 1856; Kendall, *History of New Orleans*, I, 197.

[60] *Daily Crescent*, June 13, 1856.

[61] *Ibid.*, June 5, 1856; Overdyke, "History of the American Party in Louisiana," *loc. cit.*, XVI, 420.

little concern to themselves. An endeavor to stir them to action by the reminder that the Democratic party had always stood behind them proved futile, for in a postelection comment, the editor noted that, as a result of intimidation and disinterest, foreigners had not voted.[62]

The presidential campaign of 1856 proved the extent to which the Americans had become the political masters of New Orleans. When the campaign opened, circumstances indicated a Democratic victory. In 1852, for the first time in twenty years, the Democrats had won the city, partially because their platform was favorable to the South. It guaranteed the finality of the Compromise of 1850, and the time had come when such guarantees were all-important to the South. In 1856 the Democratic platform was even more prosouthern than in 1852; it endorsed the Kansas-Nebraska Act and recognized southern aims in Cuba and Central America. The Whig party, traditional rival of the Democrats, had been replaced by the American party, which was only two years old by the time of the election. Nevertheless, in 1856 the city gave the American candidate, Millard Fillmore, 5,858 votes out of 8,333. This was a majority of 3,500, the largest ever given a presidential nominee in New Orleans.[63] Fillmore did not get Louisiana's electoral vote, however; James Buchanan had a 1,400 majority in the state.

The Democrats described the election as a day of fraud and a reign of terror carried through successfully by the Americans. On several nights before the election Know Nothings disguised by false whiskers and blackened faces circulated throughout the city, assaulting naturalized citizens to keep them from the polls on election day. A mob of masked men attacked the Carrollton Railroad station on St. Charles and Felicity, beating the workmen and driving them from the building.[64] On election day bands were reportedly circulating with their hands wrapped in handkerchiefs con-

[62] *Daily Orleanian,* June 1, 6, 1856.
[63] Owen, "Presidential Elections," 48.
[64] Follett, "The History of the Know Nothing Party in Louisiana," 74.

cealing brass knuckles or slings. They thronged the streets near the polls and either frightened away or assaulted the Democratic voters. On former occasions they usually had gone after the insignificant foreigners, but now such men as Supreme Court Justice Thomas Slidell and J. J. McCormick, a prominent citizen, were attacked. Chief Justice Slidell was knocked senseless by a blow from a ruffian armed with brass knuckles. His health was never restored, and he died in 1860 in a sanatorium as a result. It was said that after one o'clock in the afternoon few Democrats were allowed to approach the polls, much less to vote.[65]

The techniques employed by the Know Nothings were again successful, for the Democratic vote decreased 50 per cent from the 1852 election.[66] The feud between Pierre Soulé and John Slidell for control of the Louisiana Democratic party is sometimes assigned as the reason for the small Democratic ballot. This rivalry had been a thorn in the side of the state Democratic party since the 1840's. During Soulé's absence as foreign minister to Spain, Slidell and his "oligarchy" tightened their control over the party. When Soulé returned and saw what had happened, the bitterness between him and Slidell heightened. Antagonism between the two wings of the party steadily increased, offsetting advantages that might have accrued from the decline of the Whigs.

The Americans attributed the low Democratic vote to a boycott by the anti-Slidell wing of the party. These Democrats did not vote for Buchanan since they knew that Slidell would be the power behind the throne. Such glib explanations by no means account for what actually happened. Probably many Democrats did boycott the election, and it is true that the Soulé Democrats disliked Buchanan. But in 1852 Winfield Scott was even more unpopular with the Fillmore Whigs; yet the decrease in the Whig vote in 1852 was slight compared to the Democratic decrease in 1856. At

[65]*Ibid.*, 75; *Louisiana Courier*, November 5, 1856; *Commercial Bulletin*, November 5, 1856; Henry P. Dart, *John Blackstone Cotton, 1824–1881* (New Orleans, 1915), 16.

[66]Owen, "Presidential Elections," 48.

most, only a few hundred votes were lost by the boycott. The Soulé–Slidell rivalry was not strong enough in 1856 to account for such a one-sided vote. Although the rivalry was statewide, there was no comparative decline in the Democratic vote outside of New Orleans.[67]

Although the rise of the Know Nothings and the Soulé–Slidell feud both influenced the presidential election of 1856 in New Orleans, neither of them adequately explains the vote for Fillmore. The answer lay in the connection between New Orleans municipal politics and any national election held in the city. Here the Know Nothing party was much more than an attempt to divert the slavery issue through attacks on Catholic and immigrant. In the Crescent City it was the symbol of one of the two forces engaged in a pitched battle for political leadership. The machinery of the Americans was brought to perfection in the municipal elections of 1856, and the political organization continued to operate smoothly in the presidential election of November, though the latter had far less local importance.

The chief planks in the platform of the Know Nothing party aimed at eliminating Catholics and immigrants from American politics. In 1854 this party began its activity in New Orleans. In its inception there, it followed the lead of the parent organization—it was anti-Catholic and anti-immigrant. In the city at that time Catholicism was generally confined to the area below Canal Street, Protestantism to that above. Naturally, the Know Nothings at first were considered an "uptown" party.

Coincidentally, Canal Street also separated the Creole and American sections of New Orleans. These two cultural groups had been battling each other for political power almost since the Louisiana Purchase. Although the American sector had outstripped the Creole in numbers and wealth, circumstances had put it in a politically inferior position by 1854. The Whig party, which most of the Americans supported, collapsed. Besides having their party disintegrate, Americans saw their

[67] *Ibid.*, 81, 82.

opponents, the Creoles, switch over in large numbers to the Democratic party, in order to make full use of the daily increasing immigrant vote. The Americans adopted desperate measures to relieve their seemingly hopeless situation. Capitalizing on the secrecy that surrounded early Know Nothing activities, they used the party to disfranchise their political opponents by terroristic methods. By the end of 1856 they had so succeeded in capturing the government and politics of New Orleans that they dropped the secrecy and made overtures to both Catholic and immigrant. They welcomed all who would accept American leadership. At the time when the party was on its deathbed in almost every other part of the country, it was achieving its most outstanding success in New Orleans.

CHAPTER FIVE

# *Holding the Line*

BY the summer of 1856 the Know Nothing party of New Orleans was everywhere victorious. No one could "be so blind as not to see that Americans will rule," said an organ of the American party in the Crescent City.[1] In another area, too, the Creoles were losing out rapidly. The year 1857 marked the first appearance of Comus, which signalized the end of Creole control of Mardi Gras. In its inception Comus was entirely American; not a single Creole was among its first members.[2] Even a year earlier the Creoles recognized their defeat when they lamented, "The good old Creole customs are rapidly falling into disuse, as the people of the Second District go down before the men of Maine and Massachusetts, who have succeeded in controlling the 'business' of the city to a great extent in a narrow space of ground between Bienville Street and Felicity Road."[3] In politics the Creole section of New Orleans did not so readily admit the superiority of the Anglo-Saxon municipality; but the Americans, through the Know Nothing party, had secured a dominance that was permanent.

The victories of "Sam" in 1856 alarmed the Democrats throughout the state. The Democratic governor, R. C. Wickliffe, in his message to the state legislature for 1857, announced that one-third of the voters in New Orleans had been denied the right of suffrage. He spoke of "that secret political organization which arose in our midst to divide our people ac-

[1] *Semi-Weekly Creole*, June 7, 1856.
[2] Perry Young, *The Mistick Krewe* (New Orleans, 1931), 67.
[3] *Daily Delta*, February 6, 1856.

cording to the accident of religion or birth. . . . It is a well-known fact that at the last two general elections many of the streets and approaches to the polls were completely in the hands of organized ruffians. . . . Thus, nearly one third of the voters of New Orleans had been deterred from exercising their highest and most sacred prerogative."[4] Later in the year he observed that "these facts demonstrate that some extraordinary cause was at work to prevent a large proportion of lawful voters from enjoying the sacred franchise."[5]

This "extraordinary cause" was the methods in use by the Americans to insure their control of the city's government.[6] The Democrats feared a decrease in the majorities by which they controlled the state. If such a trend continued, it would be only a matter of time until Louisiana was lost to the party.[7] This fear was in reality unfounded. After the stinging defeat the Know Nothing party received in the 1856 presidential election,[8] the national council met at Louisville and recommended that each state adopt such a platform as it deemed best. This was the end of the Native American party in most of the nation and in Louisiana, except for New Orleans.[9]

Nevertheless, the governor asked the state legislature for a law which would right the wrong, and it complied by passing the Election Bill of March, 1857, which provided New Orleans with a central board of election. Composed of the mayor, attorney-general, registrar of voters, and two additional citizens of the city to be appointed by the governor, this board was to appoint commissioners to conduct the elections and to preside at the polls. Separate from the board, an office of superintend-

[4]Quoted in Follett, "The History of the Know Nothing Party in Louisiana," 78. See also John S. Kendall, "The Municipal Elections of 1858," *Louisiana Historical Quarterly*, V (July, 1922), 362.

[5]Quoted in Overdyke, "History of the American Party in Louisiana," *loc. cit.*, XVI, 608.

[6]*Daily Picayune*, June 5, 1856.

[7]Overdyke, "History of the American Party in Louisiana," *loc. cit.*, XVI, 608.

[8]The American party received 25 per cent of the popular vote, but only 2 per cent of the electoral vote.

[9]Follett, "The History of the Know Nothing Party in Louisiana," 77.

NEW ORLEANS in the 1850's

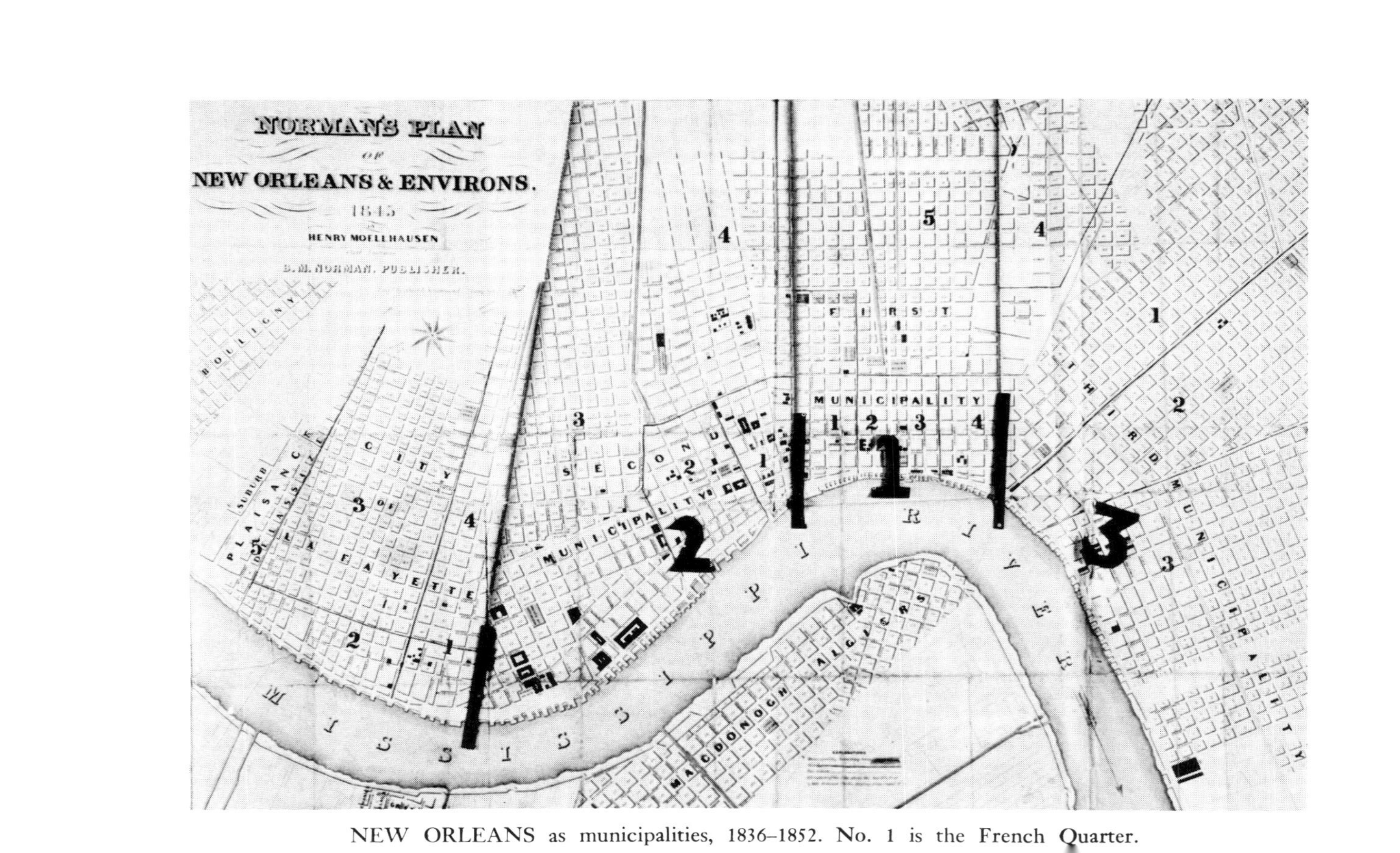


NEW ORLEANS as municipalities, 1836–1852. No. 1 is the French Quarter.

NEW ORLEANS as districts, after 1852. No. 2 is the French Quarter; No. 4 is the former City of Lafayette (Felicity to Toledano streets).

LAFAYETTE SQUARE in the 1850's—scene of Fort Defiance, 1858

JACKSON SQUARE in the 1850's–scene of Fort Vigilance, 1858

*Collection of Leonard V. Huber*

GERARD STITH, Mayor of New Orleans, 1858–1860—a member of the typographers' union.

JOHN T. MONROE, Mayor of New Orleans, 1860–1862—a former stevedore and member of the stevedores' union.

*Collection of Leonard V. Huber*

PARADE OF COMUS—The Americans, precluded from the gay Mardi Gras balls of the Creoles, started their own "Krewe" in 1857. There was not a single Creole in the first "Mystick Krewe of Comus." This sketch, from the *London Illustrated News* of May 8, 1858, shows the second Parade of Comus on Mardi Gras of that year.

ent of elections was created. This officer could deputize as many men as he wanted and could arrest anyone without a warrant on suspicion that a breach of the peace was contemplated. He, too, was appointed by the governor. The deputies could not be arrested by any local or state force during the election, since all civil power was suspended. Citizens would be required under severe penalty to serve as deputies. The city of New Orleans was to be responsible for all expenses incurred by the board.[10] Anyone attempting to interfere with the commissioners of election would be liable to arrest by the superintendent. The attorney-general was to receive personally 20 per cent of the fines imposed for violations of the election act.[11]

Americans labeled the bill revolutionary and damned it as "wild, misguided, tyrannical legislation."[12] "If the Legislature of Louisiana," stormed the *Daily Crescent*, "suppose, or any members thereof suppose, that the free born, independent, intelligent and honest citizens of this metropolis are going to submit to the unparalleled, uncalled for and outrageous tyrannies proposed by this bill–that they will tamely truckle to the abrogation of right of trial by jury and consent to a revival of the atrocious system of imprisonment for debt–they are woefully mistaken. The future, under any and all circumstances that may arise, can have nothing in store for us half as bad as this bill proposes to inflict upon us."[13] To the Americans nothing could have been worse than having the city revert to Democratic control–a likely prospect if the bill were completely carried out.

Apparently the act was entirely the work of Slidell and his

[10]*Louisiana Session Laws, 1857* (Baton Rouge, 1857), 277; Overdyke, "History of the American Party in Louisiana," *loc. cit.*, XVI, 608; *Daily Crescent*, March 5, 14, 1857.

[11]Overdyke, "History of the American Party in Louisiana," *loc. cit.*, XVI, 609; Follett, "The History of the Know Nothing Party in Louisiana," 79.

[12]*Daily Crescent*, February 26, 1857.

[13]*Ibid.*, February 27, 1857. The *Bee* and the *Daily Picayune* also condemned the bill, though in less violent language.

wing of the Democratic party, for the Soulé group condemned it in strong language, saying, "Give blood money to a public officer, and he invariably sinks into a bloodsucker."[14] Undoubtedly the two wings of the Democratic party split further apart after the presidential election of 1856. Slidell engineered the Buchanan boom from its very beginning and emerged from the election with absolute control of federal patronage in Louisiana.[15] Soulé followers were coming to prefer the continuance of American rule to that of Slidell.[16]

The regular Democrats hailed the bill as "an imperative necessity." Those who objected to it had "indulged in such severity of language, and [had] appealed so directly to baser passions in opposing it, as to surprise anyone not familiar with their open or tacit approval of or connivance at the very outrages the proposed act is intended effectually to prevent." The Creoles hoped the bill would restore the vote to those thousands who had been deprived of it.[17]

American Mayor Charles Waterman immediately announced that he would not serve on the election board, as he thought it unconstitutional. Before the bill could be put into operation the Know Nothings had a chance to conduct another election on their own terms. In April, 1857, New Orleanians chose six judges for the district courts of the city, an important election to the American party since it was these judges who naturalized the immigrants. The Know Nothings were successful in placing their candidates in each of the six district courts. They rejoiced over having stopped the wholesale manufacture of votes for at least four years.[18]

The Democrats hoped that the new election law would

[14]*Daily Delta*, February 26, 1857.

[15]L. M. Sears, *John Slidell* (Durham, 1925), 141–42.

[16]The two groups of the Democratic party grew daily more irreconcilable. The complete defeat suffered by Soulé in 1856 was the beginning of a rapprochement between his branch of the Democratic party and the Know Nothings. *Daily Delta*, February 26, 1857.

[17]*Louisiana Courier*, February 26, 27, 1857.

[18]Overdyke, "History of the American Party in Louisiana," *loc. cit.*, XVI, 609–10; Follett, "The History of the Know Nothing Party in Louisiana," 80.

function by the time of the aldermanic elections of June, 1857, for it was useless for them to participate in an election in New Orleans without outside help. Since the new board was not yet ready to operate, the Democratic powers decided not even to nominate candidates. The editor of the *Daily True Delta*, an uptown Democratic organ, was so incensed over this decision that he boldly charged that the Democratic party in New Orleans was controlled by the downtown "Exchange Alley Squad." All of the uptown delegates attended the nominating convention, but only one member from below Canal Street. They wanted to put up a ticket, but when they realized that to do so would openly split the party, the uptowners backed out. The next day the "Exchange Alley Squad" announced their intention not to participate. The furious uptown Democrats wanted the state Democracy to know just what conditions prevailed in the party in New Orleans.[19] For the first time the press openly betrayed the party alignment by district, which had been accomplished about five years earlier.

With no opposition the Know Nothings easily placed all of their candidates, though only two thousand votes were cast throughout the whole city.[20]

On July 21, 1857, Mayor Waterman obtained an injunction from Judge H. B. Eggleston of the first district court prohibiting the election board from functioning.[21] Immediately he was accused by the Democrats of having waited for a recess in the supreme court, enabling the Americans to bring their case before a district court.[22] The mayor answered that he had refused to sit on the election board for two months and that the Democrats had had plenty of time to bring the case to court. Nevertheless, Waterman's attempt to defeat the bill failed, for on October 13, Judge John B. Cotton, the Democratic superintendent of elections, enjoined the mayor from naming polling places and thereby forced him to withdraw

[19] *Daily True Delta*, May 31, 1857.
[20] *Daily Crescent*, May 28, June 4, 1857.
[21] *Ibid.*, July 23, 1857.
[22] *Louisiana Courier*, July 23, 1857.

Judge Eggleston's injunction.[23] For the city to have an election, the board must function. The New Orleans Democrats themselves did not have much faith in the bill. As the campaign for the November state and congressional canvass opened, the city Democrats warned the country parishes that they must act as if not a single vote would be polled for the Democrats in the city.[24] Such an announcement was an indication of Know Nothing power in New Orleans.

The attorney-general of Louisiana was in favor of meeting force with force. In a letter referring to the operation of the election law in New Orleans, he openly stated that the police of the city were wholly inefficient and that a grand jury report showed that they were unable to suppress the election riots. He felt that the remedy could be found in "the superior power of the state." The legislature should organize an armed force for elections in New Orleans. Exclusively under the control of state officers, it would be strong enough to subdue all opponents and have the physical and legal means to arrest all disturbers of the peace. Any half-way measure would inspire contempt and provoke opposition. The force should have ample authority and be fully capable of controlling and conquering all possible resistance. He insisted that the expense of the measure be paid entirely by the taxpayers of the city.

The Americans were determined that the election law should not operate as the attorney-general intended. As they explained it, the special deputies of the superintendent of elections were to receive ten dollars a day, but the extraordinary deputies, as they were called, were to get no pay. The special deputies, the Americans said, were all Democrats, while the extraordinary deputies were Americans. Only the paid special deputies would turn out on election day. The Americans would have none of it.[25]

As the off-year November election approached, the Democrats pinned their hopes on the election law, and each party ran a full slate of candidates for the state legislature and Con-

[23]*Daily Crescent,* July 26, October 14, 1857.
[24]*Ibid.,* October 24, 1857.
[25]*Ibid.,* October 31, 1857.

gress. The Democratic nominees were all chosen by Slidell, since his wing of the party dominated the state convention.[26] In the election only 5,464 out of a possible 12,640 voted. The Know Nothings again carried the day by reducing the size of the Democratic vote; the decimation of voters in this election was worse than before. For the first time in reporting returns, the American mouthpiece, the *Daily Crescent*, did not total the statistics from the various wards and precincts. The figures from the second and third districts were so disproportionately low that even the *Crescent* was embarrassed by the totals.[27]

Outside New Orleans the Democratic ticket was completely victorious. In the state senate there were twenty-three Democrats and nine Know Nothings. The house was divided forty-nine to thirty-eight. This gave the Democrats a majority of twenty-one votes on a joint ballot.

In the congressional elections only the first district, New Orleans below Canal Street and Plaquemines and St. Bernard parishes, elected a Know Nothing. George Eustis, the incumbent, was returned. In the second district, New Orleans above Canal Street and parts of the sugar parishes, the Know Nothings lost by less than one hundred votes. The first congressional district was virtually a pocket borough of New Orleans, but the city had trouble controlling the second, for often the New Orleans vote was offset by the country parishes. Throughout the rest of the state Democrats won by a majority of 4,649.[28] The election proved conclusively that the Know Nothing party was dead in Louisiana except for New Orleans.

The Creole effort to regain the city through use of the election law was fruitless. In November, 1857, the Americans refused to co-operate with the superintendent of elections, Judge John B. Cotton. They would not serve as deputies, sell arms or ammunition to the board, or answer summonses.

[26]Follett, "The History of the Know Nothing Party in Louisiana," 82.
[27]*Daily Crescent*, November 3, 1857.
[28]Overdyke, "History of the American Party in Louisiana," *loc. cit.*, XVI, 614.

Cotton tried to hire some three thousand deputies, offering them ten dollars a day at the expense of the city.[29] But the American party had no intention of permitting the election bill to jeopardize its position. The Democrats admitted that the election was peaceful, but it was a peace of terror. If the American "thugs" had found it to their interest, they would have rioted and murdered as they always had. The Creoles also had bitter words for those Democrats who did not see to it that the election bill functioned; they urged that it be made usable at the next election.[30]

The year 1857 was no better for the Creoles than 1856 had been. Their efforts to use the state legislature to alleviate their condition came to nought. Formerly, the legislature had been a successful instrument in managing local affairs, as in 1853 when the Democrats had changed the charter in order to get control of the police force. The election bill was a similar move. This time, however, the strategy failed. Even if they had to defy state law, the Americans were determined that the Creoles would not regain possession of New Orleans politically.

By 1858 the time was ripe for another independent movement in New Orleans. When one of the major parties found itself in a hopeless predicament and had not won any elections for several years, such a movement usually appeared. To continue to use the defeated party's name seemed to invite further failure. The New Orleans Democrats had not won an election for over three years and chances of success were growing slimmer. Besides, Christian Roselius and a group of two hundred former Whigs in the summer of 1857 announced their dissatisfaction with the American party. They hoped for a revival of the Whig party. The Know Nothings had become too violent and were guilty of graver abuses than those they sought to remedy. While expressing sympathy with the Americans, "for the most part of our family," Roselius thought it had gone beyond the means of legitimate redress

[29]*Daily Crescent,* November 7, 1857.
[30]*Ibid.,* November 5, 1857.

and had become the aggressor.[31] Such malcontent was grist for an independent mill.

By early summer, 1858, conditions were even more propitious to the success of an independent movement. The American party was split by the withdrawal of the moneyed element.[32] Led by Charles M. Waterman, this group represented the mercantile interests of New Orleans who had lived in the city for many years. After the municipalities were consolidated, they supported the Know Nothing party as a means of securing power for the Americans. By 1858 this group was not able to control the party any longer. It was now in the hands of the ward clubs, located in neighborhoods inhabited by workingmen who had moved to New Orleans in the last ten or fifteen years. These clubs met weekly, and the American press carried the notices of each, urging attendance.[33] This element did not hesitate to use violence to achieve political success. It was probably they who dressed as Indians, paraded through the streets intimidating Democratic voters, and made the American party the party of thugs. Increasingly, the Know Nothings depended on and courted this element.

Such proceedings were heartily disliked by the wealthier members, though they desired American control of New Orleans and were not above election trickery in order to achieve it. But when they lost power and violence mounted, they left the party. "Men who embraced, three or four years ago, Know Nothingism as a political principal," said the *Daily True Delta*, "abandon it now, that they find it to be only the embodiment of a huge crime, and if their convictions in regard to what constituted the first basis of that secret organization have undergone little change, they have at least been convinced that the mode by which it was sought to make them successful must be abandoned."[34]

When the American nominating convention met, the Water-

[31]Follett, "The History of the Know Nothing Party in Louisiana," 81.
[32]*Bee*, May 27, 1858. [33]*Daily Crescent*, May 1–30, 1858.
[34]*Daily True Delta*, June 1, 1858.

man forces were outnumbered and withdrew. Calling themselves Independents, they met in a suite in the St. Charles Hotel, from which the "vulgar masses [were] excluded,"[35] and nominated for mayor, P. G. T. Beauregard, superintendent of the customs house. Though a Creole, Beauregard was acceptable, for he had been educated in the "progressive spirit" of the Americans. He had been sent to New York instead of to Europe for his education.[36] The Democrats, because of intraparty strife, put up no candidate but generally supported the Independents.

The American party nominated Gerard Stith for mayor. Born in Virginia in 1821, he came to New Orleans as a young man to work as a printer for the *Daily Picayune*. In 1858 he was foreman of the composing room, a job to which he returned after his term as mayor.[37] The nomination of Stith symbolized the new orientation of the American party toward labor. One of the basic issues of the campaign was the claim that Beauregard was against the working classes. "Mechanics and laborers will not vote for him," said the *Daily Crescent*. He was accused of having replaced white labor at the customs house with Negro slaves. Further, it was asserted that Beauregard was a Democrat before becoming an Independent and that the Democrats had recently voted against labor legislation in Baton Rouge. Throughout the campaign the Americans repeatedly charged the Independents with having the wealth, but not the quality, of the city in their ranks.[38] The Americans were making a strong effort to gather the workingmen into their party.

Before either ticket was announced, the Creole-immigrant coalition decided to do something about the way elections were conducted in New Orleans. Lower New Orleans did not intend to tolerate further intimidation and disfranchise-

[35]*Daily Crescent*, June 2, 1858.

[36]R. T. Beauregard, "A Sketch of General G. T. Beauregard," *Louisiana Historical Quarterly*, II (July, 1919), 276.

[37]Kendall, *History of New Orleans*, I, 224–25.

[38]*Daily Crescent*, May 31, June 1, 2, 1858.

ment at the hands of the Americans. In March a Vigilance Committee was formed with the ostensible purpose of guaranteeing a peaceful election in the city. Since the rank and file were composed of Creoles and persons of Irish and German extraction, the term "peaceful election" to them meant Democratic opportunity.[39]

The Vigilance Committee was by no means synonymous with the Independent movement. The former was a downtown group. When New Orleans became virtually two armed camps during the campaign, members of each were identified as belonging to the *uptown* or *downtown* division.[40] The Independent movement, however, was not exclusively uptown or downtown. It was more an attempt of the wealthy to wrest the government of New Orleans from what they called the "thugs" or rabble of the Know Nothing party.[41] Know Nothings readily admitted that the members of the Independent movement were wealthier than those of the American party.[42] The *Commercial Bulletin*, uptown champion of the Independents, labeled the Vigilance Committee illegal and refused to support it.[43] Nevertheless, the Creole Democrat Beauregard reportedly "entered into an agreement" with the Vigilance Committee.[44]

At three o'clock on the morning of June 3 the state arsenal in the Cabildo was seized by two hundred armed men calling themselves "Vigilants." Providing themselves with arms, ammunition, and cannon and encamping in Jackson Square, they took possession of the lockup, police headquarters, and the courtroom of the sixth district court. Guards were posted, and no one was admitted to the camp. The names of individual members were never revealed, although their leader was known to be Captain John Duncan, attached to the Marine Hospital

[39]Kendall, "The Municipal Elections of 1858," *loc. cit.*, V, 366; *Daily Crescent*, June 8, 9, 1858.

[40]*Bee*, June 4, 1858.

[41]*Commercial Bulletin*, June 4, 1858.

[42]*Daily Crescent*, June 2, 1858.

[43]*Commercial Bulletin*, June 4, 1858.

[44]Reinders, "A Social History of New Orleans, 1850–1860," I, 139.

in New Orleans. On the same day in the *Louisiana Courier* appeared the following notice: "Having resolved to free our city of the murderers who infest it, we have assumed its temporary government, ready to account to our God and to the laws of our country for the acts we are about to perform. We have no political object in view, and we call upon all true and good men to join us in the work we have undertaken. . . . We will and shall have order and security. . . . We shall inflict prompt and exemplary punishment upon well known and notorious offenders . . . and shall not lay down our arms until this is effected." This manifesto was signed by "The Vigilance Committee."[45]

The city was alarmed the next morning to find an armed fort in its midst. Even the noncommittal *Daily Picayune* declared that civil war was imminent, if something were not done. In the editor's opinion the civil authority had been usurped by the Vigilance Committee, an unlawful body, and bloodshed was almost sure to follow. He failed to see how the brute force of armed soldiery could produce a fair election.[46]

Meanwhile, the number of men encamped in Jackson Square increased, reconverting it literally into a *Place d'armes*. In the words of an out-of-town observer, "The arsenal building was crowded with men, all wearing intelligent countenances and a determined air, while the minie muskets are being brought out and stacked conveniently for instant use; the brass twelve pounder ready for dreadful deeds, with its mouth pointing so as to sweep Chartres Street, down to Canal with grape, and the gunners with their ammunition besides it; the cordon of sentinels (in citizen's dress but each armed with a minie musket) extending completely around Jackson Square, with the dense throngs of inquisitive persons pressing up against the line of sentinels, all tending to give it a look of anything but a peaceable city."[47]

[45] *Louisiana Courier*, June 3, 1858. [46] *Daily Picayune*, June 4, 1858.
[47] Overdyke, "History of the American Party in Louisiana," *loc. cit.*, XVI, 615, quoting from the Baton Rouge *Weekly Gazette and Comet*, June 3, 1858.

The mayor's first move after hearing of the Vigilance Committee's action was to convene the city council, which assembled at ten o'clock on the morning of June 3. The first proposal of that body was to arm the people and disperse the Vigilants by force. This would have meant a serious conflict, for the Vigilants had fortified their camp with granite blocks torn up from Chartres Street. Mayor Waterman refused, therefore, to issue the proposed proclamation, and the council passed a resolution demanding his resignation. If he should resign, H. M. Summers, a former recorder and now a senior alderman and president of the board of aldermen, would become the mayor. It was generally understood that Summers was prepared to carry out the wishes of the council and that he opposed the renomination of the mayor. Waterman refused to resign, and the council did not press impeachment at this time. Instead, they invested the mayor with discretionary powers, and the meeting adjourned.[48]

The excitement caused by the news of the Vigilance Committee's action was by no means confined to the council chamber, for while the meeting was in progress within the city hall, a large mob had formed in Lafayette Square. It was addressed by a Mr. Poindexter of the *Daily Picayune*, who assured them that the mayor and council would handle the emergency. He also insisted that the American party was the party of law and order. Obviously the Americans expected battle with the Vigilants, as hundreds of citizens began to gather arms and engage in military drilling, preparing to attack should the mayor issue the order. That night, Thursday, June 3, afraid that the Vigilants would attempt to take possession of the city hall, the Americans stationed guards all around it.[49]

Mayor Waterman's next step was a trip down to Jackson Square accompanied by Benjamin G. Harrison, who had been an Independent candidate for mayor before Beauregard was

[48]Kendall, "The Municipal Elections of 1858," *loc. cit.*, V, 366–67; *Daily Picayune*, June 4, 1858.

[49]Follett, "The History of the Know Nothing Party in Louisiana," 88; Kendall, "The Municipal Elections of 1858," *loc. cit.*, V, 367; Overdyke, "History of the American Party in Louisiana," *loc. cit.*, XVI, 616; *Daily Picayune*, June 4, 1858.

named. Waterman suggested to Captain Duncan that the Vigilance Committee immediately disband. Duncan refused unless the mayor would deputize the whole committee to serve as special police until after the election. Waterman answered that he did not have authority to take such action, and the meeting ended. The mayor returned to the city hall, where an announcement of his action was made to the assembled crowd.

When this meeting with the Vigilants bore no fruit, Mayor Waterman decided to call out the militia. Orders were sent to General John L. Lewis, former Democratic mayor and now commandant of the troops and inspector of elections. He posted the notice tardily, and it elicited no response. At the same time Mayor Waterman signed a requisition for weapons and issued a warrant for the arrest of Duncan and the committee, charging them with being unlawfully armed. The city's chief of police delivered the papers to Jackson Square but returned "feeling somewhat ridiculous," for he was completely without means to carry out the arrest.

By the afternoon of June 3 the apparent inaction of the city officials began to be criticized, and a meeting of fifteen men, supposedly of no particular political bias though all of the names were American, was held at the St. Charles Hotel. Two committees were appointed, one to call on the mayor and one to call on the Vigilants, to try to reconcile their differences. These committees apparently accomplished nothing.[50]

On the morning of June 4 the mayor again visited the Vigilant headquarters, this time with General Lewis. A two-hour conference followed, in which an attempt at compromise was made. Waterman accepted Duncan's earlier demand that the Vigilants be sworn in as a special police force until after the election. Duncan informed the mayor that the Vigilants would not give up their position in the state arsenal until they had been sworn in.[51] It was at best questionable for a city offi-

[50]Kendall, "The Municipal Elections of 1858," *loc. cit.*, V, 367; *Daily Picayune*, June 4, 1858.

[51]Follett, "The History of the Know Nothing Party in Louisiana," 80.

cial to accept demands made by a group virtually in revolt against the city government, but Waterman explained his action on the basis of his sincere desire to avert bloodshed and also upon the lack of a precedent in dealing with the matter.[52] Upon his return to the city hall he informed the public of his action, and immediately an unfavorable demonstration arose. Contrary to the mayor's order, a portion of the mob secured two cannon and set off to attack "Fort Vigilance," as Jackson Square had come to be called. When the column reached Canal Street, a shot was fired, apparently by an excited onlooker, and half of the group dispersed. The other half continued into Royal Street, where the barricades of the Vigilants made the futility of their efforts obvious. They returned to Lafayette Square, where they disarmed and stored the weapons in the city hall.[53]

Americans were becoming increasingly alarmed over the Vigilance Committee's deliberate attempt to overthrow the constituted authority of New Orleans.[54] All the mayor had done about it was to accept a compromise, the conditions of which were dictated by the lawbreakers. Waterman, as chief executive of the city, was held responsible for the lack of action taken by the government, and threats of violence were circulated against him personally. Rumors that he felt more at home in the Vigilant camp did not increase his popularity uptown. Fortunately, a heavy rain fell, and the mob around the city hall left. By this time the Know Nothing newspapers had begun to condemn Waterman for his inaction, calling it an attempt to legalize treason.[55] Again his explanation was his desire to avert bloodshed.

[52]Francis G. Burns, "Charles M. Waterman, Mayor of New Orleans, His Defense of His Conduct in the Municipal Election of 1858," *Louisiana Historical Quarterly*, VII (July, 1924), 468.

[53]Kendall, "The Municipal Elections of 1858," *loc. cit.*, V, 369; *Bee*, June 5, 1858; *Daily Picayune*, June 5, 1858.

[54]The Vigilants even announced they would publish a list of those who deserved an "ignominious death, if they are taken." *Daily True Delta*, June 5, 1858.

[55]Kendall, "The Municipal Elections of 1858," *loc. cit.*, V, 369; *Daily Crescent*, June 5, 1858.

On the afternoon of June 4 the mayor returned to Jackson Square for another meeting with Duncan, whom he was unable to see until four o'clock in the morning. According to his own statement, he had had no rest for forty-eight hours and fell asleep from exhaustion. This was the reason he gave for his extended stay in the "enemy's" camp.[56] Possibly he no longer felt safe in his own section of the city. During the day of Saturday, June 5, he was visited by an uptown delegation, which attempted to persuade him to return in order to swear in special police because of the collapse of the regular force. He was urged either to return or to resign so that some sort of positive action could be taken. Waterman compromised and deputized Gerard Stith, recorder of the first district and Know Nothing candidate for mayor, to swear in a police force. The delegation returned to the city hall, and Stith began to recruit. Meanwhile, Waterman's advisors informed him that he could not legally delegate his power as head of the city's police, and he in turn informed Stith that his appointments were void. Since he had already sworn in some sixteen hundred men, all Americans, Stith disregarded the rescinding order.[57]

The council met at 6:00 P.M. on June 5 to give Waterman a chance to explain what he had done. The mayor was not present at the opening of the meeting but instead had sent a message asking whether he would receive protection if he should leave Jackson Square. Party feeling against him was mounting. The council delegated Stith to assure the mayor of his safety. Waterman accompanied Stith as far as the St. Charles Hotel, where he refused to go any farther upon being

[56]Burns, "Charles M. Waterman, Mayor of New Orleans, . . . ," *loc. cit.*, VII, 474–76.

[57]Kendall, "The Municipal Elections of 1858," *loc. cit.*, V, 370; *Daily Crescent*, June 5, 1858; *Bee*, June 7, 1858; *Louisiana Courier*, June 6, 1858. The *Courier* published a statement by a citizen who declared that when he presented himself to Recorder Stith to enroll for the special police force he was asked his name. Upon answering, he was promptly taken off to a corner and asked if he were connected in any way with the American party, or if he had at least voted American, and whether he intended to vote American. When he refused to commit himself for the coming election, he was hustled out of the room.

informed that an unruly mob had again assembled in front of the city hall. Incensed by his action, the assistant board of aldermen immediately presented impeachment articles, charging him with deserting his post, attempting to legalize an unlawful organization, refusing to enforce the laws and ordinances of the city, and generally jeopardizing the lives and property of the citizens of New Orleans. By the terms of the city charter Waterman was automatically suspended as soon as the articles were brought against him. The council appointed Summers, president of the board of aldermen, to act as mayor. Summers promptly issued a proclamation ordering the Vigilance Committee to disband, but the order was completely ignored.[58]

By nightfall on Saturday, June 5, New Orleans was divided into two armed camps. Downtown was Jackson Square—Fort Vigilance—while uptown was the city hall and Lafayette Square—Fort Defiance. The city took on an appearance of siege, and bullet-proof shirts were advertised in the papers. Arrests were made by both camps,[59] and each sent out scouting parties on the night of June 5. The Vigilants overhauled some of their opponents, but the only casualties were their own scouts who were mistaken for the enemy. Four men were killed, and nine wounded. The Vigilants did not attempt to go beyond the neutral ground on Canal Street, another indication of the sectional nature of the conflict.[60]

Sunday, June 6, found the city fairly quiet, although there were reports that shots could be heard from various parts of the city. Rumors of attack "flew thick and fast" from both camps.[61] The chief of police abandoned his post and left the city for his home in the country, reportedly under the influ-

[58]Kendall, "The Municipal Elections of 1858," *loc. cit.*, V, 371; Proceedings of the Common Council, June 5, 1858 (City Archives, New Orleans Public Library, New Orleans); *Daily Picayune*, June 6, 1858; *Bee*, June 7, 1858; *Daily Crescent*, June 7, 1858.

[59]*Bee*, June 4, 1858.

[60]Follett, "The History of the Know Nothing Party in Louisiana," 92–93; Kendall, "The Municipal Elections of 1858," *loc. cit.*, V, 372.

[61]*Daily Crescent*, June 7, 1858.

ence of a $3,000 bribe.[62] Some of the propertyholders and merchants tried to devise a plan to persuade the Vigilants to disarm, disperse, and co-operate with the civil authorities in order to secure a peaceful election. The Vigilants declined, and the proposal was dropped.[63]

On the day of the election, Monday, June 7, both sides continued to hold their forts. The disturbing influences so much in evidence at other elections did not present themselves.[64] The certainty that violence would be met with violence doubtless contributed to the quiet.[65] The party press cautioned the Americans to "bear and forbear, until forbearance ceases to be a virtue." The *Daily Crescent* admitted that the men on the Independent ticket were able but claimed that, if they were elected, Slidell would be mayor of New Orleans.[66]

Although the election bill of 1857 was still in effect, it did not have any marked influence on this contest. In view of the state of affairs in the city, the vote was surprisingly large. The results showed an American party victory in most of the city. Their candidate for mayor, Gerard Stith, was successful. Americans were elected recorders in all of the districts except the second (Creole) where L. S. Forstall, the Independent candidate, won the contest. In that district Independents also won places on both the board and the assistant board of aldermen. Throughout the rest of the city, American party candidates were victorious with the exception of two assistant aldermen, one from the first district and one from the third. The number of votes in the second and third districts remained lower than it had been in the pre-1856 period, an indication that intimidation was still practiced. The American party again carried the third district. It was said that the Know Nothings sent vagabonds claiming to be Irish and German citizens into the back precincts "to lie, bully and intimidate

[62] *Bee,* June 7, 1858; *Daily Crescent,* June 7, 18, 1858.

[63] Kendall, "The Municipal Elections of 1858," *loc. cit.,* V, 372; *Daily Crescent,* June 7, 1858.

[64] *Daily True Delta,* June 9, 1858.

[65] *Bee,* June 8, 1858.

[66] *Daily Crescent,* June 7, 1858.

voters." The district had been "overawed" in the election.[67] Had the Independents carried it, they probably would have won the election.[68]

The Vigilants circulated about the polling places throughout the day, but the election was peaceful. By nightfall they had abandoned their camp, and Duncan announced the return of arms to the arsenal. By the next day the Committee had completely disappeared, having spent about $30,000 in five days. During this time five men had been killed and nine or ten wounded. The city sued Duncan and the Committee for $6,-000 damages to the courtroom and records. A few of the Vigilants were arrested, but no serious effort was made to punish them. Many left the city for "health trips," and some fled to the swamps only to be driven out by hunger.[69] After the election the Americans recommended amnesty for members of the Committee, for they felt that the individuals who took part in it were, for the most part, respectable but misguided. The new government took no serious action against the Vigilants.

The *Daily Crescent* considered the Know Nothing victory unparalleled in view of the confusing issues which the party faced. Among these was the strategy of the Independent party in placing on its ticket many respectable names intended to attract old-line Whigs, Democrats, and all elements hostile to the American party. The expenditure of large amounts of money by the Independents and their constant agitation that all the city's evils were caused by the American party were also important factors. In addition to these handicaps, the Know Nothings had to overcome federal and state influence which was on the side of the Independents.[70]

The usual cries of fraud were heard after the election. Cre-

[67]*Daily True Delta,* June 1, 12, 1858.

[68]*Daily Picayune,* June 10, 1858.

[69]Kendall, "The Municipal Elections of 1858," *loc. cit.,* V, 373–74; *Daily Crescent,* June 9, 1858.

[70]*Daily Crescent,* June 8, 1858; Overdyke, "History of the American Party in Louisiana," *loc. cit.,* XVI, 618. At this time state and federal patronage was controlled by the Democrats.

oles cited three polls at which a total of thirty-nine votes for Beauregard had not been counted, and they complained of the scarcity of Independent ballots at the polls. They said the election had been awarded to a set of candidates by a group of election commissioners who thwarted the wishes of the people.[71]

The formation of the Vigilance Committee in 1858 was the climax of the Creole-American struggle for political mastery of New Orleans. After this episode resistance was tacit, and the Americans easily retained their hold on municipal and state politics in the city. The Independents, however, springing as they did partially from a breakup within the Know Nothing party itself, continued to participate in elections for the next two years, but they never materially disturbed the reign of the Americans. Superior political organization overcame even the wealth of the new opposition.

The election of 1858 convinced the Creoles that further battle against the Know Nothings was futile. The Americans were growing in numbers, and their powerful political machine was even embracing former opponents in the second and third districts. In Gerard Stith, the Creoles said, the city had a mayor whom the better classes could respect. They expressed confidence in his ability to rescue New Orleans from the deplorable condition it had been in for the last two years. Though they did not agree with his politics, if he were "fearless and faithful," none would be readier to do him honor.[72]

The year 1858 was also the climactic one for the New Orleans Know Nothing party. Long since dead throughout most of the country and even in the rest of Louisiana, the party in the city had to contend with a split which saw the secession of many of its wealthier members. It also faced an armed organization whose real purpose was to rid the city of the party. It met all of these challenges and emerged with as tight a control as ever, although after 1858 the party was in the hands of a new group responsive to labor. This group was the party's

[71] *Louisiana Courier,* June 8, 12, 1858.
[72] *Ibid.,* June 22, 1858.

source of strength. Through the tight-knit organization of its labor members in the various wards it was able to achieve the dominance of New Orleans. Neither the Democratic party nor the renegade Americans and Democrats in the Independent movement could uproot the Know Nothings.

CHAPTER SIX

# New Wine in Old Bottles

THE Independent movement of 1858 was the most serious threat encountered by New Orleans Know Nothings. Their success in meeting the challenge insured the city a Native American administration for two more years. But nationally the party was dead after its failure to elect Fillmore in 1856, and by 1859 it was practically dead in Louisiana, except in New Orleans where it had been taken over by labor. This isolation forced the party to face the critical problem of deciding on its candidates for the congressional and gubernatorial contests of 1859 and the presidential election of 1860.

George Eustis, American congressman from the first congressional district (downtown New Orleans and St. Bernard and Plaquemines parishes), announced in May, 1859, that it was no longer feasible for him to seek his re-election on the Know Nothing ticket. The few party members who were still in Congress, he said, were either going over to the Republican party in the North or were sustaining defeat after defeat in the South. Attempts to revive the Whigs were futile, for their members had gone off into other parties. Even the staunch Whig supporter, the *Bee*, admitted that the effort to reanimate the organization was "utterly abortive." Eustis concluded in most cases the southern representatives had no choice but to join one of the factions of the Democratic party. The coming contest would be Democrats versus Republicans–North versus South. Since the South had no choice but to stand with the Democrats, he decided to join them without delay.[1]

[1]*Daily Crescent,* May 16, 1859.

While the rest of the South was rapidly turning to the Democratic party, it was impossible for New Orleans Know Nothings to do this, for the Democratic party there had been the political foes of the Americans. Therefore, in state and national contests the local party had to form a coalition.

Coincidentally with the approach of this dilemma for the Americans came the climax of the Slidell-Soulé feud. Since 1848 these two had been battling each other for control of the Louisiana Democratic party. In that year Soulé defeated Slidell by maneuvering votes in the state legislature and won the United States senatorship. In the early 1850's, however, Soulé accepted appointment as minister to Spain, which left his senatorial seat vacant. Slidell, who became boss of the Democratic party after his rival's departure, obtained the senatorship. Thus, when Soulé returned from Spain in 1853, he found Slidell completely in control of the party in Louisiana. Thereafter Soulé attempted to wrest the leadership from Slidell by one means or another without openly splitting the party. In all of his efforts he failed.

Developments in 1859 gave Soulé an opportunity to break openly with Slidell and the Louisiana Democratic party. Because the state Know Nothing party was moribund, Soulé knew the time was ripe for an opposition party which could also include the New Orleans Americans. His bitter rivalry with John Slidell led him to disrupt the state Democratic party. Although Soulé favored the candidacy of Stephen A. Douglas while Slidell supported James Buchanan, politics in Louisiana had little to do with the abstraction of popular sovereignty or congressional control of slavery.[2]

Once Soulé decided on an open break with the Slidell forces, his strategy was to act first. Instead of waiting until May 16, 1859, the date set for election of delegates to the state Democratic convention of May 25, he ignored the state central committee and called an open meeting in Odd Fellows Hall for April 4. His speech was plainly a bid for American support.

[2]Mary Lilla McLure, "The Elections of 1860 in Louisiana," *Louisiana Historical Quarterly*, IX (October, 1926), 614.

The meeting elected Soulé Democratic delegates to represent the city.[3]

The state convention turned out to be solidly in the hands of Slidell. The Soulé wing of the party met with total defeat,[4] withdrew, and formed the Opposition ticket. They nominated Thomas J. Wells of Rapides Parish for governor and John Ray of Ouachita Parish for lieutenant-governor. The regular Democrats chose Thomas O. Moore, a planter of Rapides Parish, for governor.[5]

The New Orleans Know Nothings accepted the advances of Pierre Soulé and supported the Opposition ticket for state officers. In the parish elections, however, the American party put up its own candidates for congressman from the first congressional district, sheriff, coroner, tax assessors, clerks of court, state tax collector, board of state assessors, justices of the peace and constables, and members to the state legislature.[6]

Having solved the problem of finding a slate to support in the state election, the New Orleans Know Nothings were again plagued with internal dissension. By October, 1859, a segment of the party led by Charles P. Dreaux expressed dissatisfaction with the nominees for sheriff and clerk. It withdrew and formed the Independent American ticket. Dreaux had been offered a place on the Opposition ticket but refused it; he was displeased because he had previously been passed over by the Know Nothings in earlier campaigns. His defection looked like a Slidell trick. In return for the support of Slidell's Democrats in the municipal election, Dreaux's Independent American ticket, if elected, was allegedly to support Benjamin in the legislature. At a public meeting of the Independent Americans on Canal Street, Judge John B. Cotton, the main speaker, was

[3]*Ibid.*, 620; *Daily Crescent*, April 5, 1859.

[4]Van D. Odom, "The Political Career of Thomas Overton Moore, Secession Governor of Louisiana," *Louisiana Historical Quarterly*, XXVI (October, 1943), 985–87.

[5]James Kimmins Greer, "Louisiana Politics, 1845-1861," *Louisiana Historical Quarterly*, XIII (July, 1930), 452, 456.

[6]*Daily Crescent*, November 7, 1859.

known to be a staunch Slidell man.[7] The Independent American ticket put up a slate of candidates for sheriff, district attorney, coroner, clerks of court, and all the regular parish offices.[8]

On November 7, election day, New Orleans voters were confronted with four tickets: the regular Democratic and the Opposition tickets for state offices, the Independent American and the American tickets for parish and local offices. The Americans supported the Opposition (state) and American (local) tickets, which included an American candidate for congressman from the first congressional district. The regular Democrats supported the Democratic (state) and Independent American (local) tickets, including a regular Democrat for the first congressional seat. Despite the four tickets, there were actually only two coalitions: one consisting of the American and Opposition parties, the other of the regular Democrats and the Independent Americans.

In New Orleans the election was very quiet, as only about half of the registered voters went to the polls. The Democrats and Independent Americans were completely defeated in the city, and the Know Nothings elected their whole parish ticket, including a congressman, three state senators, eighteen state representatives, and all of the parish officers. The Opposition ticket also carried New Orleans by a majority of 1,312 but won only one other parish in the state, Terrebonne. Carrying the rest of the state, Democrat Moore was elected by a majority of 10,166 votes, the largest ever given a candidate in Louisiana history.[9]

Although Slidell's Democratic party was in full control of the rest of Louisiana, the Know Nothing party was still

[7]McLure, "The Elections of 1860 in Louisiana," *loc. cit.*, IX, 637; *Daily Crescent*, October 25, 1859.

[8]Follett, "The History of the Know Nothing Party in Louisiana," 100. See also Overdyke, "History of the American Party in Louisiana," *loc. cit.*, XVI, 622.

[9]Follett, "The History of the Know Nothing Party in Louisiana," 101–102.

supreme in New Orleans. For all positions for which the Americans ran or supported candidates, they were victorious by between one and two thousand votes. The party relied on the same procedure as it had for the past several years to secure its victory—intimidation of the Democratic vote. As usual, in the Democratic downtown sections of the city the vote was disproportionately small.

In the race for congressman the same pattern was repeated. Americans elected their candidate from the first congressional district but could not win the second district, which included uptown New Orleans and parts of the sugar parishes.[10]

Although by 1860 politics in New Orleans revolved mainly around the dilemma facing the South if Abraham Lincoln were elected, the administration of local affairs was still a necessity. As June approached, the city was forced to turn its attention to the business of electing a mayor and other municipal officials. At this point another split occurred in the American party, the result of which was the Citizens' ticket, composed of renegade Know Nothings. Many of the wealthier members had abandoned the party in 1858 because control had slipped from their hands. All of the moneyed group did not withdraw at that time, however, thinking they would regain their leadership in 1860. When the time came for selecting delegates to the city nominating convention, the Know Nothing officials in the city government had themselves chosen. Thereupon the moneyed faction rebelled, claiming that according to party usage twelve months should elapse before an officeholder could be eligible as a delegate to the nominating convention. These rebels, "substantial" men of the city who represented "that conservatism which is the surest guarantee of good order and quiet in our civil administration," formed the Citizens' ticket. Among the bolters was the *Daily Crescent* itself, staunchest advocate of the American party in the city. Orthodox Know Nothings said the reason for the desertion of the *Crescent* was that its proprietor, J. O. Nixon, one of the founders of the party, was

[10] *Ibid.*

among those frustrated by not having been nominated for an aldermanic post. This Nixon hotly denied in the columns of the *Crescent.*[11]

The regular Americans nominated for mayor John T. Monroe, a stevedore who had been a resident of the city for about twenty years. He had long been a labor leader, and "over the working classes his control was never broken."[12] The Citizens' ticket, headed by L. H. Place, a rich merchant, could foresee only misfortune if Monroe and his slate were elected. "We are threatened with bad government—inexperienced, indiscreet, if not unscrupulous men, are aspiring to the control of the affairs of the corporation—there is actual danger of bad government ahead."

The regular American party chided the Citizens for advocating change when, for so many years, they had campaigned against it. The Citizens answered that they were not advocating change. Businessmen and merchants were the backers of the Citizens' ticket, and it was this group which had founded the American party. Now that the regular Americans were increasingly responsive to the labor element, the Citizens asserted that it was they themselves who most truly represented the original spirit of the American party. On election day the Citizens admonished the businessmen and merchants to get to the polls to protect their own ticket.[13]

Besides Monroe and Place, Alexander Grailhe was also a candidate for mayor on an Independent ticket, which was the label chosen for the old Creole Democrats in the mayoralty campaign of 1860. Before Grailhe was tendered the Independent nomination, it was apparently offered to a Dr. J. S. McFarlane. According to the Democratic Creole *Louisiana Courier*, the offer came from many of "the most prominent citizens of the city." Although he rejected the nomination,

[11]*Daily Crescent,* May 15, 21, 22, June 2, 1860.

[12]Kendall, *History of New Orleans,* I, 228; "Biographies of the Mayors of New Orleans, 1803–1936" (typewritten copy, New Orleans Public Library [New Orleans: Works Progress Administration, 1939]), 61.

[13]*Daily Crescent,* May 24, 26, June 4, 1860.

McFarlane said that if he were elected, "every office (qualification considered) which I could control would be given to the 'ancient population,' " which was "being rapidly excluded from place, power, or official station."[14] By 1860 there was by no means complete fusion of the two cultures. The Creoles had been shoved aside. They probably realized this, but it was still difficult for them to accept their decline.

To the American party, however, the problem in June, 1860, was not Creoles but dissension within its own ranks. Again the tightness of the party's organization and the loyal support of the working classes served it well, and the Know Nothings retained control of the administration. Monroe was victorious in all except the fourth district, but the vote reflected a sectional allegiance. Place, the renegade American running on the Citizens' ticket, received 1,014 to Monroe's 1,370 in the first district. Grailhe, the Independent (Democratic-Creole) candidate, received only 459. In the second (Creole) district, Grailhe ran close to Monroe—840 to 916, while Place polled only 246. In the third district Monroe led the other two combined almost two to one. Place won the fourth district with 523 to Monroe's 463, while only 224 cast their ballots for Grailhe.[15]

The returns in all of the districts except the first suggest changes in the political organization of New Orleans. The first district was, as expected, divided between the Americans, with a few Independent (Democratic) ballots. In the second, the reappearance of an opposition is noteworthy. Monroe defeated Grailhe by only seventy-six votes. Apparently the American party no longer felt the necessity of intimidation. The coalition between Soulé and the Know Nothings in 1859 probably produced a rapprochement between the second district and the American party. Besides, the anti-Catholic and anti-immigrant nature of the party had disappeared soon after the Know Nothings succeeded in dominating the city. The size of the American vote in the third district reflected the

[14]*Louisiana Courier*, June 1, 1860. [15]*Daily Crescent*, June 6, 1860.

progress of the Know Nothings in wooing the workingmen.[16] Probably the choice of Stith and Monroe as heads of the party did much to win over the immigrants, for with workingmen as mayors their interests were better represented than they had ever been in the Democratic party. The regular Americans lost the fourth district because it was increasingly populated by rich citizens who moved to the area now known as the Garden District.

While the New Orleans American party was experiencing internal dissension which, in the end, could have resulted in its disintegration, like other southerners local citizens faced a serious national emergency in which the stakes were much higher. This was the decision as to their course of action should Abraham Lincoln be elected. The national crisis vastly overshadowed local elections and the plight of the American party. As a party issue in New Orleans, however, the presidential election of 1860 was not very important. Before the Charleston convention the New Orleans Know Nothings were willing to support Douglas, or any other candidate the national Democratic party might select, as the best way to defeat the Republicans. The disruption of the Democratic party at Charleston marked the end of the national organization as far as local Know Nothings were concerned; a Baltimore compromise was unlikely. To prevent secession most Know Nothings transferred their support to the Constitutional Union party.[17] John Bell, a former Whig who was nominated as its candidate, received most of the American party vote and easily carried the city. For the first time in many years local party lines and personalities took a back seat in a New Orleans political campaign.[18]

By January, 1861, Louisiana was out of the Union, and poli-

[16]For example, in 1858 the American *Daily Crescent* ran a long series of articles in praise of the German *Volksfest. Daily Crescent,* May 10, 17, 18, 1858; Reinders, "A Social History of New Orleans, 1850–1860," II, 462–63.

[17]Owen, "Presidential Elections," 112–13.

[18]*Ibid.,* 88.

tics was relegated to a position of insignificance. Columns of the local press that were once filled with political arguments for or against some party were now devoted to war news and diatribes about northern fanaticism. The total lack of any political comment made it seem as if southerners were afraid that opposition among themselves might be mistaken for lack of unity.

In New Orleans elections between secession in January, 1861, and the invasion of the city in April, 1862, the Southern American party[19] was the only one that maintained uninterrupted identity. In the aldermanic contest of June, 1861, it was generally unopposed, although there were some Independent candidates. The Southern Americans elected eleven out of fourteen.[20] In the campaign for parish officers, members to the state legislature, and Confederate congressman in November, 1861, there were three tickets. Besides the Southern American, the Citizens' ticket reappeared; there was also a third, the Confederate. In only one newspaper in the city was there any electioneering. The *Daily True Delta*, still violently anti-American, accused the Southern American party of having originated in the hated North.[21] The rest of the press merely presented all tickets and said nothing about any. It was generally agreed that the days of party nomination were gone and that the Citizens' and Confederate tickets were composed of gentlemen who wished to run for office, not candidates supported by a party. The day of the split ticket had arrived; aspirants to office would be chosen on the basis of personal interest and friendship instead of partisan considerations.[22]

The election of November 4, 1861, was the last in which the Southern Americans participated. By this time the party had undergone such basic changes that it was hardly recognizable as the Know Nothing organization of 1855 and 1856. In a card signed by one of the supporters of John P. Walden,

[19]The name used by the Know Nothings after secession.
[20]*Daily Crescent*, June 4, 1861.
[21]*Daily True Delta*, June 3, 1861.
[22]*Bee*, November 4, 1861; *Daily True Delta*, November 5, 1861.

the Southern American candidate for sheriff, the signer insisted that Walden had never been a Know Nothing. Obviously, there was a sharp difference in 1861 between being a Southern American and a Know Nothing.[23]

The election itself produced a strange development in New Orleans. The Southern American party won most of the parish offices, but only because of its large majorities in the second (Creole) and third (immigrant) districts. In most wards of the two American districts, the first and fourth, the Citizens' ticket polled as many votes as the Southern American, if not more.[24] Since the Citizens were mainly renegade Southern Americans, the men of politics elected in the first and fourth were not Democrats, but former Know Nothings. Nevertheless, for the organization which had reduced the Creole and immigrant districts of the city almost to political impotence to turn to them for survival is one of the greatest ironies in the history of the party. The issue among Americans, Creoles, and immigrants was settled. The American party ended its days as the standard-bearer of a new cause—labor.

[23]*Daily True Delta*, November 3, 1861.
[24]*Ibid.*, November 5, 1861.

# *Epilogue*

The death of the Whig party and the influx of immigrants might well account for the brief appearance of the Know Nothing party in New Orleans as a temporary refuge for former Whigs. Most southerners within a year or two found a place in the Democratic ranks, which soon came to symbolize the South. New Orleans did not fit this pattern and the Know Nothing party prevailed—the result of circumstances, not of political issues.

After partial successes in 1855 and the early part of 1856, most Louisiana Know Nothings abandoned "Sam" and, with the exception of the abnormal conditions that existed during reconstruction, for the rest of the century the state was controlled by the Democratic party. Unchallenged Democratic ascendancy in Louisiana actually began in 1854. In New Orleans, however, the same year marked a decline that was to last until after the Civil War. In the Crescent City a combination of incidents, all within a two-year period, made possible the continuance of the Know Nothing party.

Progress had been made in settling the differences between the Creoles and Americans. Intermarriages and general social intercourse were common by the 1850's. To the casual observer, 1852 might even be cited as the year when the breach between the two was healed, for the city was then reunited after a fourteen-year separation. But consolidation raised a question which had lain dormant during separation: who would control municipal politics? In 1836 the Creoles, of course, were the dominant political force in the city, but by 1852 the Americans were outstripping them in numbers. Members of the "ancient population," whose life spanned both dates, were aware of the threat to their supremacy.

At the time of these developments in the municipal organization of New Orleans international forces were at work which would affect city politics. The potato famine in Ireland and the revolutions in Europe drove thousands of immigrants to the United States. By 1860 New Orleans had received over 54,000, and in the early 1850's the vast majority of them joined the Democratic party. This group could easily hold the balance of political power.

The Creoles realized that, if they shifted their support to the Democratic party, they could use the immigrant vote and perhaps control New Orleans. By 1853 the Americans knew what was happening but could do little about it, since their own Whig party had fallen to pieces nationally and locally. The coincidence of these events enabled the Know Nothing party to strike deep roots in New Orleans, where it became much more than the ephemeral organization it was in other parts of the country. Locally it was more than a temporary outburst of indignation against immigrants and Catholics, since it provided an outlet for the traditional American opposition to the Creoles.

From 1855 until after the Civil War the Democrats had little influence on the administration of local affairs. New Orleans Know Nothings did not go over to the Democratic party because it represented the coalition which the Americans bitterly opposed. This explains why Pierre Soulé, longtime opponent of John Slidell, could not muster enough strength for an opposition movement before 1859. By that year the Know Nothings had established absolute control of New Orleans, as their success in meeting the crisis presented by the Vigilance Committee of the preceding year proved. Soulé wooed the regular Americans because of their strength.

Throughout its history in New Orleans the strategy of the Know Nothing party was based on expediency, not on principles. Just as a combination of events made possible the rise of the party, the flexibility of its political tenets insured its continuance. In its inception the organization was avowedly anti-Catholic. Yet almost immediately such Catholics as Charles Gayarré were admitted. Apparently the party convinced him that the Louisiana wigwam did not accept the religious plank of the national platform. Nine months later he resigned his membership and advocated immediate dissolution of the party because of its proscription of Catholics. But as far as New Orleans Know Nothings were concerned, anyone was welcome who wished to join. Their sole object was to crush the Democratic coalition. After the triumphs of 1855 and 1856 they admitted to their ranks Creoles, Catholics, immigrants—in fact, all who would support the new regime.

The course pursued is somewhat analagous to that of a revolutionary government which uses any means possible to gain power. The slightest sign of opposition was ruthlessly crushed. When the new order was secure in its position, former opponents were allowed to come into the fold without being persecuted. The high-sounding platform of the Know Nothings did not stop them from using a remedy, intimidation, which was worse than the prevailing evil—fraudulent voting.

The ability of the Know Nothing party to adapt itself to circumstances was epitomized in the changes which resulted in the naming of such men as Stith and Monroe to the mayoralty. In 1855 the control of the party by a wealthy "aristocracy" almost lost Huffty the nomination for sheriff because he was a "mere shop-keeper."[1] By 1860 the same party had elevated a former stevedore to the position of mayor of New Orleans. The crisis which had made almost all of uptown and some of downtown New Orleans willing to unite under the leadership of an "aristocracy" was over. The Democratic coalition was suppressed to the point where it almost ceased to exist. The Know Nothings had built a powerful machine which now drew most of its strength from the workingmen's ward clubs. After the crisis passed, this labor element

[1]Follett, "The History of the Know Nothing Party in Louisiana," 37.

realized the potential of its numbers and rebelled against the leadership of the moneyed class. In the end each group put up a separate ticket.

Together, they were the same men who had won the battles of 1855 and 1856. But after the split of 1858 the regular American party saw a chance to strengthen itself by appealing to a segment of the population throughout the city which could bolster its prospects through sheer weight of numbers. Otherwise, the splinter group might use their wealth to recapture political office. Accordingly, the regular party shifted its emphasis to a program that would attract labor. The strategy worked, and New Orleans elected Gerard Stith, the first mayor to regard such matters as health and education as responsibilities of the city. The flexibility which allowed the Know Nothings to turn their attention to a popular platform enabled them to maintain their identity even when the stress of war had eclipsed all other party lines.

It was no accident that the last two prewar mayors of New Orleans were skilled workers, representing the only two trades which had formed strong local unions. The fight between Creole and American aristocrats made leaders of the workingmen realize the political power of the masses, and in the end they took control of the new party away from the wealthier elements. When the Federals sought to erect a civil government on the basis of labor votes during the occupation, which began in 1862, they were not using a new technique but accepting rather the realities of the local political situation. The liberal features of the Constitution of 1864 followed as a natural consequence, and Michael Hahn became the first Free State governor in the same year, largely because of his popularity with laboring groups.[2]

Nationally the Know Nothings were a third party which served as a bridge by which Southern Whigs became Democrats and Northern Whigs Republicans. In New Orleans the role of "Sam" was quite different, for the Know Nothings remained the dominant party until the outbreak of the Civil

[2]Shugg, *Origins of Class Struggle in Louisiana*, 114–15, 198–200, 207–10.

War, and in the process labor emerged as the controlling political force.

# Selected Bibliography


## NEW ORLEANS NEWSPAPERS

*Bee-L'Abeille*, 1850–1862.
*Commercial Bulletin, Price Current, and Shipping List*, 1850–1862.
*Daily Crescent*, 1849–1862.
*Daily Delta*, 1850–1862.
*Daily Orleanian-L'Orleanais*, 1850 through April 18, 1858.
*Daily Picayune*, 1850–1862.
*Daily True Delta*, 1850–1862.
*Die Deutsche Zeitung*, 1854.
*Louisiana Courier-Courier de la Louisiane*, 1850 through November 24, 1860.
*Semi-Weekly Creole*, October 4, 1854, through June 30, 1856.
*Weekly Delta*, 1850–1862.

## OFFICIAL DOCUMENTS

Cable, George Washington. "New Orleans, Historical Sketch," *Report on the Social Statistics of Cities*, George E. Waring, Jr. (comp.). (United States Bureau of Census, *Tenth Census of the United States: 1880*, XIX, 213–67.) Washington: Government Printing Office, 1887.

*Journal of the Constitutional Convention, 1845*. New Orleans, 1845.

*Louisiana Session Laws, 1804–1856*.

Proceedings of the Common Council, 1850–1862. City Archives, New Orleans Public Library.

United States Bureau of Census. *Seventh Census of the United States: 1850. Statistical View of the United States. . . Being a Compendium of the Seventh Census. . .*, by J. D. B. DeBow. Washington: Government Printing Office, 1854.

United States Bureau of Census. *Eighth Census of the United States: 1860. Population*, I. Washington: Government Printing Office, 1864.

## MEMOIRS, PAPERS, AND TRAVELERS' ACCOUNTS

Ampère, J. J. *Promenade en Amerique; États Unis-Cuba-Mexique.* 2 vols. Paris, 1855.

Gayarré, Charles Étienne Arthur. *Address to the People of Louisiana on the State of Parties.* New Orleans, 1855.

Hall, Abraham Oakey. *The Manhattaner in New Orleans.* New York, 1851.

Ingraham, Joseph H. *The Sunny South, or the Southerner at Home, Embracing Five Years' Experience of a Northern Governess in the Land of the Sugar and the Cotton.* Philadelphia, 1860.

Kingsford, William. *Impressions of the West and the South During a Six Weeks Holiday.* Toronto, 1858.

Lyell, Sir Charles. *A Second Visit to the United States of North America.* 2 vols. London, 1849.

Olmsted, Frederick Law. *The Cotton Kingdom, A Traveller's Observations on Cotton and Slavery in the American Slave States.* Edited by Arthur M. Schlesinger. New York, 1953.

Pfeiffer, Ida. *A Lady's Second Journey Round the World.* New York, 1856.

## BIOGRAPHIES

"Biographies of the Mayors of New Orleans, 1803–1936." Typescript, New Orleans Public Library. New Orleans: Works Progress Administration, 1939.

Butler, Pierce. *Judah P. Benjamin.* Philadelphia, 1907.

Mercier, Alfred. *Biographie de Pierre Soulé, Senateur à Washington.* Paris, 1848.

Sears, Louis Martin. *John Slidell.* Durham, N. C., 1925.

## PERIODICALS

Beauregard, R. T. "A Sketch of General G. T. Beauregard," *Louisiana Historical Quarterly*, II (July, 1919), 276–81.

Burns, Francis P. "Charles M. Waterman, Mayor of New Orleans, His Defense of His Conduct in the Municipal Election of 1858," *Louisiana Historical Quarterly*, VII (July, 1924), 466–79.

Dart, Henry P. (ed.). "Autobiography of Charles Gayarré," *Louisiana Historical Quarterly*, XII (January, 1929), 5–32.

Evans, Harry Howard. "James Robb, Banker and Pioneer Railroad Builder of Ante-Bellum Louisiana," *Louisiana Historical Quarterly*, XXIII (January, 1940), 170–258.

Greer, James Kimmins. "Louisiana Politics, 1845–1861," *Louisiana Historical Quarterly*, XIII (July, 1930), 444–83.

Kendall, John S. "The Municipal Election of 1858," *Louisiana Historical Quarterly*, V (July, 1922), 357–76.

Kmen, Harry. "New Orleans' Forty Days in '49," *Louisiana Historical Quarterly*, XL (January, 1957), 25–45.

McLure, Mary Lilla. "The Elections of 1860 in Louisiana," *Louisiana Historical Quarterly*, IX (October, 1926), 601–702.

Odom, Van D. "The Political Career of Thomas Overton Moore, Secession Governor of Louisiana," *Louisiana Historical Quarterly*, XXVI (October, 1943), 975–1054.

Overdyke, W. Darrell. "History of the American Party in Louisiana," *Louisiana Historical Quarterly*, XV (October, 1932), 580–88; XVI (January, 1933), 84–91 (April, 1933), 256–77 (July, 1933), 409–26 (October, 1933), 608–27.

Reinders, Robert Clemens. "The Louisiana American Party and the Catholic Church," *Mid-America*, XL (New Series, XXIX [October, 1958]), 218–28.

Reinders, Robert Clemens. "Orestes A. Brownson's Visit to New Orleans, 1855," *Louisiana Historical Quarterly*, XXXVIII (July, 1955), 1–19.

## *SECONDARY WORKS*

Castellanos, Henry. *New Orleans as It Was.* New Orleans, 1895.

Curtis, Nathaniel C. *New Orleans: Its Old Houses, Shops and Public Buildings.* Philadelphia, 1933.

Kendall, John S. *History of New Orleans.* 3 vols. New York, 1922.

King, Grace Elizabeth. *Creole Families of New Orleans.* New York, 1921.

McGloin, Frank. "History of New Orleans," *Biographical and Historical Memoirs of Louisiana.* 2 vols. Chicago, 1892. I, 159–219.

Overdyke, W. Darrell. *The Know Nothing Party in the South.* Baton Rouge, 1950.

Shugg, Roger W. *Origins of Class Struggle in Louisiana: A Social History of White Farmers and Laborers During Slavery and After, 1840–1875.* Baton Rouge, 1939.

Tinker, Edward Laroque. *Creole City, Its Past and Its People.* New York, 1953.

Young, Perry. *The Mistick Krewe: Chronicles of Comus and His Kin.* New Orleans, 1931.

## *UNPUBLISHED THESES AND DISSERTATIONS*

Adams, Ben Avis. "Indexes of Assimilation of the Creole People in New Orleans." M.A. thesis, Tulane University, 1939.

Briede, Kathryn C. "A History of the City of Lafayette." M.A. thesis, Tulane University, 1937.

Follett, Edith Chalin. "The History of the Know Nothing Party in Louisiana." M.A. thesis, Tulane University, 1910.

Owen, Merlin Elaine. "The Presidential Elections of 1852, 1856, and 1860 in New Orleans." M.A. thesis, Tulane University, 1957.

Reinders, Robert Clemens. "A Social History of New Orleans, 1850–1860." 2 vols. Ph.D. dissertation, The University of Texas, 1957.

# Index

2588-B, 1-62